QUILTED
ONE BLOCK
MARVELS

CAROLYN SULLIVAN

Quilted One Block Marvels

By Carolyn Sullivan

American Quilter's Society
PO Box 3290
Paducah, Kentucky 42002-3290

Located in Paducah, Kentucky, the American Quilter's Society (AQS) is dedicated to promoting the accomplishments of today's quilters. Through its publications and events, AQS strives to honor today's quiltmakers and their work and to inspire future creativity and innovation in quiltmaking.

Editors: Karen Fail and Megan Fisher
Design, Layout and Illustrations: Susan Cadzow of Red Pepper Graphics
Cover Design: Luba Bosch
Photography: Photographix
Cover Quilt: **Underneath the Arches** – by Carolyn Sullivan

Library of Congress Cataloging-in-Publication Data

Sullivan, Carolyn.
   Quilted one block marvels / By Carolyn Sullivan.
      p. cm.
   Summary: "Learn to design your own quilt blocks by manipulating a single unit through repetition, rotation and reflection. Twelve projects with clear illustrations and instructions for basic construction. Includes tips on color and fabric selection"
--Provided by publisher.
   ISBN 978-1-57432-940-7
   1. Patchwork--Patterns. 2. Quilted goods. I. Title.

TT835.S8235 2007
746.46'041--dc22
                     2007020050

Additional copies of this book may be ordered from the American Quilter's Society,
PO Box 3290, Paducah, KY 42002-3290, or online at: www.AmericanQuilter.com.

Produced by:
QuiltWorks
Promoting Australian and New Zealand quiltmaking and quiltmakers
17 Peter Close
Hornsby Heights, NSW
AUSTRALIA 2077

Contents

Introduction

Like many people, I enjoy looking at the world around me. I see many stimulating things wherever I am, and I like to take photographs wherever I go. Photographing doors in Brussels on a trip to Belgium some years ago was a fascinating source of shapes. A visit to the Royal Botanic Gardens in Sydney yielded beautiful shapes in the lines of the shadehouse. There is a particularly appealing set of decaying garage doors in an area I visit frequently. As the doors have disintegrated, they have created the most beautiful lines that lend themselves to all sorts of design ideas. My photographs are a continuing source of inspiration for lines, shapes and colors. These are the aspects of design that most interest me. I also collect photographs from good quality magazines and beautiful books. From all of these observations, I am able to pick out particular lines and shapes that enable me to design new quilt blocks.

But designing the block itself is not enough! I also want to make interesting, exciting quilts out of them. I have played with my own blocks before for my first book, **Companion Pieces – Quilts and Embroideries**, where I concentrated on rotations of a particular block to give a whole layout for a quilt. Since then I have discovered that this is only the tip of the iceberg! There is so much more that can be done once repetition and reflection are included.

And that is what this book is about – designing your own blocks, then manipulating them through repetitions, rotations, reflections and combinations of these to make your own amazing quilts.

Fundamental to my approach to quilt design in this book is the concept of plane symmetry groups, which reduce all variants in designs with tiles (or blocks) to just seventeen options. Although only formalised in 1924, the principles have been used and referenced through the ages to create designs for wallpaper and tile patterns.

Shadehouse
page 66

I have used these symmetries in my own way particularly in simplifying the vocabulary.

I am very fortunate that I have the opportunity to teach a lot of people. I really enjoy sharing what I know and encouraging people to look at the world around them. To find their own creativity, I like to encourage people to do their own thing and to see them relish their sense of achievement. There are many techniques to assist in visualizing the world around us and to see how our own surroundings can be used to make exciting and different quilts. This book is about encouraging that creativity.

However, I know too, that many quiltmakers prefer to browse through all sorts of books and magazines and find something that they can make in their own fabrics or adapt to their own circumstances and interests. It gives me the most enormous pleasure to see quilts that I have designed reinterpreted by other quiltmakers. The projects in this book allow you to make the quilts as I have designed them or to make them with your own special characteristics. You can always change the size of a quilt. You can add more blocks or you can change the size of the block. As well as the projects, there are many layouts of my own blocks for you to choose from. This is a feast of quilts!

I hope you enjoy the feast.

My very grateful thanks:

To Ellie Harrison for quilting The Floral Quilt.

To Ken, Linda, Tim, Anthony and Norma for being there.

Designing Quilt Blocks

When designing your own blocks it is best to consider only line and shape. A quilt block needs to be relatively simple. If there are too many parts then it is difficult to piece as well as being too complicated to look at. It is hard to decide where your eye should linger. So, if the lines and shapes are simple ones, and there are only a few of them, the block itself will be simple.

There are all sorts of things to go looking for when you are thinking about design. It is a case of setting your mind to observing the world around you and looking for design possibilities. Once you have started, you will not be able to look at the world again in the same way! Look at constructions of all sorts – bridges, building sites, scaffolding, completed buildings, railway stations, road interchanges, merry-go-rounds, machinery, and so on. The natural world also offers all sorts of delights – flowers, foliage, landscape, skyscapes, animal markings.

You do not have to go on holidays to observe the world. Observations can be made in your own backyard and neighbourhood. Wherever you look, you can see shapes that will help you design interesting blocks that will, in turn, give you attention-grabbing quilts.

Sometimes in a photograph, there are many lines and shapes. So, how do you decide what might be important? Look at the photograph of Sydney Olympic Stadium during the 2000 Olympics (right). The number of lines of the construction is breathtaking but which ones will be useful?

One of the best techniques is to photocopy the photograph in black and white.

By doing this, the color is eliminated and the lines and shapes become more dominant. Decisions about color can be made later. By using a photocopy, you can also enlarge the photograph, which makes it easier to see which lines are the most useful.

Sydney Olympic Stadium

After photocopying and enlarging the image, cut a square window out of plain cardboard or paper. It is best to use cardboard that has no printing or vibrant color that will detract from the images you are trying to see. The size of the square will depend on the size of the images in the photocopy. The best way to make the decision is just to cut one! Try it out. If it works that is fine. If it doesn't, then decide whether to make the next square smaller or larger. You will probably have a very clear idea after you have made one or two. There is no rule for deciding the size of the square and it will change for different images.

Move the window in the cardboard across the photocopy until you find some interesting shapes. A colored felt-tipped pen works well to outline the square of the window onto the photocopy. You can do this as many times as you like on one photocopy, even overlapping the orange squares.

Another useful technique is to make a tracing of the enlarged black and white photocopy and then move the square over that, marking the interesting shapes as you go. The advantage of the tracing is that it is often easier to see the lines.

After outlining all of the interesting looking areas on the photocopy or tracing, it is necessary to make a tracing of each small square. You will end up with a piece of tracing paper that has many small drawings. At this stage, some of them will look very good and some you may decide to eliminate. Students

often ask which ones will be best, but once they have a number of designs in front of them, the good designs stand out!

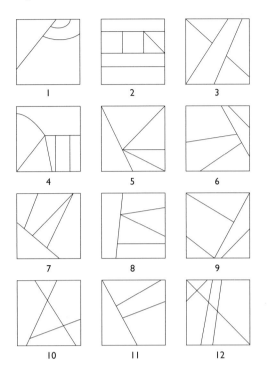

You may want to make enlargements of the good designs so that you can work with them, because they sometimes have to be adjusted. Not all designs can be easily pieced. You need to consider whether there are awkward lines that should be removed as there is no need for piecing to be difficult. Do you want curved lines? You may prefer to use straight lines only. Are there a lot of points coming to one place? This too makes piecing difficult and by moving a line a little you can make the piecing easier.

Looking at the small squares, above, you will notice that there are some that have some tricky shapes. 2 is very static and therefore not very interesting. 5 has four shapes meeting at the same point, which is difficult to piece. However, by combining the ideas of 5 and 11 with their vertical, narrow triangle and by adjusting the lines that join the triangle, I designed the **On Safari** block.

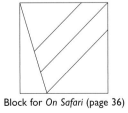

Block for *On Safari* (page 36)

So, why start with the source of inspiration in the first place, if you are going to change it? It is important to start with an image that is meaningful to you and then make the adjustments necessary to make the piecing possible – and you have designed your own block!

Sometimes it is possible to look at a photograph, select a few lines and design a new block without having to go through the whole design process. Look at the Bird of Paradise flower photograph. It is a much simpler image than the one of the complex construction of the Sydney Olympic Stadium. It is therefore possible to just look at the image and see which lines stand out.

Bird of Paradise flower

You could make a number of drawings and select from them.

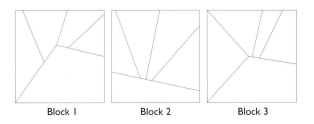

Block 1   Block 2   Block 3

Which of the three would you choose? Both Block 1 and Block 3 have a difficult area to piece in one corner. Also, they have three points joining in one place making them even harder to piece. The best choice is Block 2 because it is simpler and has no awkward joins.

could design quite a complex block if you wished, such as Block 1. Block 3 is hard to piece accurately. But, by spacing the pieces along the baseline and not joining them in one place as in Block 2, you would have an attractive, workable block.

Another matter to consider when designing a quilt block is the order in which you will piece the block. Look at the photograph of downtown Houston. There are some very powerful lines in this photograph that can be simplified into a quilt block.

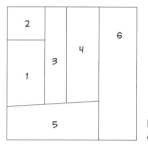

Block from
downtown Houston

Peacock

Look at the photograph of the peacock. Again, there is an obvious line at the base of the feathers with many radiating lines from the back of the peacock. You

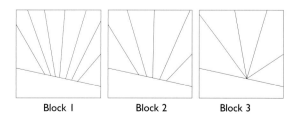

Block 1   Block 2   Block 3

Downtown Houston

Tasmanian beach scene

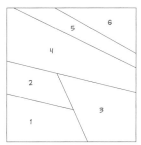

Block from Tasmanian
beach scene

Block from Sydney Harbour
Bridge

Although piece 5 is an awkward shape, it is easy to assemble the block by making the order of the piecing logical. By placing piece 1 first, followed by 2, one of the long lines has been filled. By adding piece 3, the seams of 1 and 2 are covered. Adding piece 4 completes the lines at the top of the block. Adding piece 5 covers the seams left from pieces 1, 3 and 4. Piece 6 completes the block and also covers a seam.

Another awkward shape can be seen in the drawing based on the skyscape and beach in Tasmania. Here the unwieldy shape is placed down first and then piece 2 added to it. Piece 3 covers the seams and 4 and 5 are placed down as well.

A simple block can be designed from this photograph of the supporting structure of the Sydney Harbour Bridge just by selecting the important lines. It is fine to exaggerate the slope of the line as has been done with the line between 1+2 unit and 3. This makes the design pleasing to the eye. To construct this block, lay down piece 1, then add piece 2. Adding piece 3 covers the join between 1 and 2 as well as giving a nice line on which to finish the block with pieces 4, then 5, then 6.

Sydney Harbour Bridge

While there are many things to consider when designing your own block, here are some things that are particularly important to keep in mind:

• Observe the world around you as you go about your daily life
• Keep the block simple
• Make sure the joins are uncomplicated
• Consider a logical piecing order for the block

Turning Blocks into Quilts

An old fashioned carousel using a symmetrical repeat design.

Repetition

Quilt layouts are generally based on the notion of repetition. Repeats of a single motif have been used to create beautiful and exciting patterns throughout the ages. Artists and artisans have found motifs they like – often an object they admire from the natural world – and repeated that image to make a new pattern that is admired by all who see it. The many churches, mosques and temples around the world have the most spectacular patterns that attract people to worship as well as the simple enjoyment of the building as an object of beauty. Textiles, carpets, wallpapers, tiles and mosaics are all examples of pattern used for ornamentation and decoration. Modern artists, too, use repetition to make their artwork. Andy Warhol used the image of a can of Campbell's soup very effectively by repeating it many times.

Quiltmakers also like to use repeat patterns for their quilts as the order given by the repetition of a basic block satisfies our simplest ideas of design. A basic block repeat is where the block is positioned so that each side faces the same way for each repeat. The traditional blocks that we all love and where most of us have learned our basic patchwork skills are based on the use of the repeated block.

The Ohio Star block is one that is used over and over again in many different quilts using many different layouts. A block like Ohio Star, however, appears the same whatever way you place it. It is symmetrical in all directions. If you divide it horizontally the top half is the same as the bottom half. If you then divide it vertically, all four quarters are

Ohio Star by Carolyn Sullivan using a simple repeat block design where the block is symmetrical.

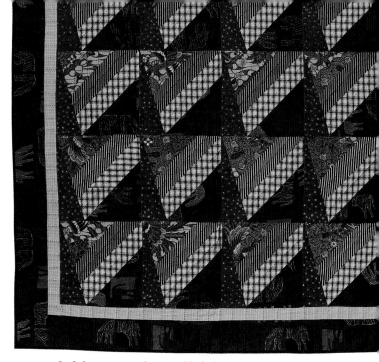

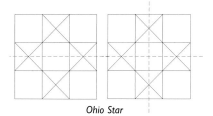

Ohio Star

identical. These lines that have been drawn on the block are called **lines of symmetry.**

If the same thing is tried with the block for *On Safari,* which was designed in the last chapter, you can see the difference. In the diagram below left, the top section of the block is different from the bottom section. In the diagram on the right, you will see that all four quarters are different. This is **asymmetry**.

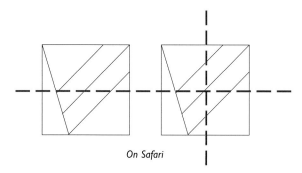

On Safari

One of the advantages of designing your own blocks is that often they are not symmetrical in the same way as the *Ohio Star*. This means that, as the block is repeated, interesting patterns emerge. Look at the repeat layout for the *On Safari* block below.

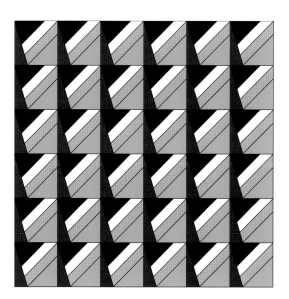

On Safari uses a simple repeat block design where the block is asymmetrical.

The tall red triangles dominate as they march across the quilt. They are eye catching and give the feeling that they make the quilt lean a bit to the left. The dark black triangles are a counter balance and lend some weight to the quilt. Compare that to the Ohio Star quilt layout below. An Ohio Star quilt, although beautiful, is not as dynamic as a quilt made from asymmetric blocks.

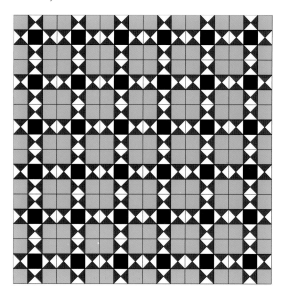

While repetition is a common feature of quilts, sometimes it is useful to change the direction of the block. This can be done in two ways – by rotation and by reflection.

Design for floor tiles incorporating rotated corner tiles.

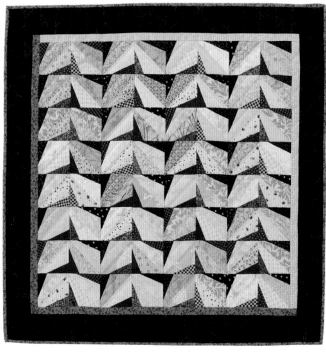

In Flight where alternate blocks are rotated 90°.

Rotation

Rotation simply means turning the block around one point. For the purposes of this book rotations are limited to multiples of 90°.

 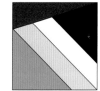

On Safari block   *On Safari* block rotated
90° clockwise

By turning it a further 90°, the block is rotated again.

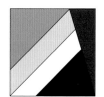

On Safari block rotated
180° clockwise

And by turning another 90°, the block is rotated again.

On Safari block rotated
270° clockwise

When all four blocks are put together, an exciting design is revealed.

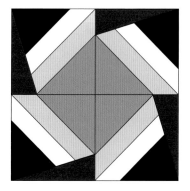

Reflection

Reflection is different to rotation. Here you need to imagine that the quilt block has been flipped over on itself. It is like the view you would get of the block if you placed a mirror in front of it. For the purposes of this book, the discussion will be limited to vertical and horizontal reflections.

Vertical reflection creates a vertical line of symmetry.

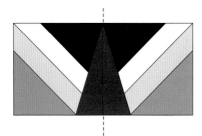

On Safari block reflected in the
vertical line of symmetry.

Horizontal symmetry is created when the block is reflected across a horizontal line of symmetry.

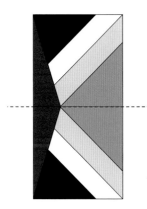

On Safari block reflected in the
horizontal line of symmetry.

This horizontally reflected block can also be placed next to the original block, creating another design variation.

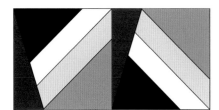

Horizontally reflected block next to
On Safari block.

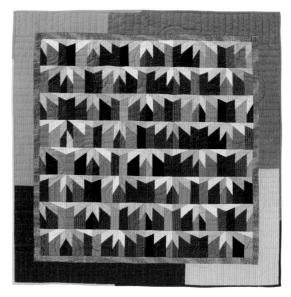

Shadehouse is designed using the block and its reflection.

It is a combination of repetition, rotation and reflection that produced the quilt layouts in this book. What follows are some suggestions that you can adopt to use your own blocks to create fabulous quilt layouts with many dynamic secondary patterns. Remember, it is repetition that is the important feature of quilt design using blocks. For most of the layouts, the unit repeated is the group of four blocks in the upper left corner. So, for the layouts given, you will see a unit of four blocks and the repetition of those four blocks. The differences in those four blocks are created by rotation and reflection.

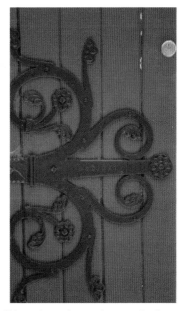

Old gate hinge showing horizontal reflection.

Group 1: Repetition

The simplest quilt layout is one where a basic block is placed in the same way in the quilt and repeated. Examples of quilts using block repetition are **On Safari** on page 36, **Palm Fronds** below and on page 30, and **The Floral Quilt** on page 56.

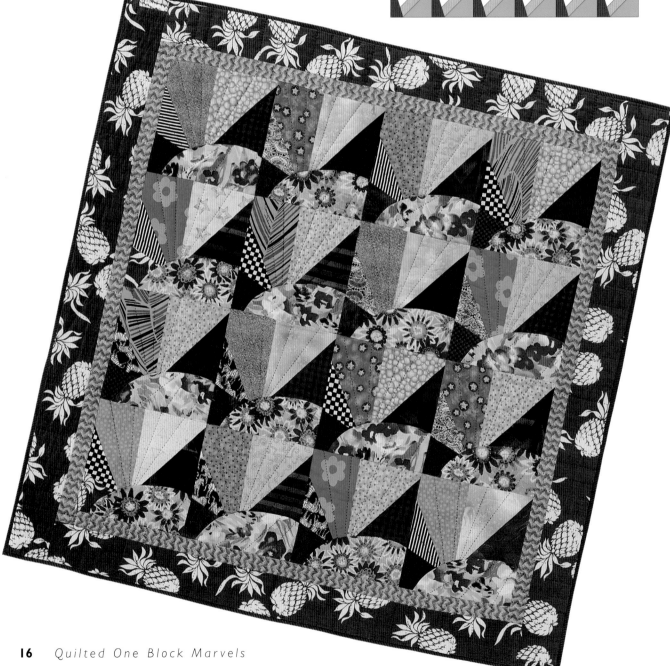

Group 2: Rotation

Rotate the basic block 180° and place it in combination with the basic blocks to create a variety of new quilt layouts.

Variation 1:

Place a **column** of the rotated blocks beside a column of basic blocks to create a new design. Look at *Red Ikat*, right, to see how this works as a full quilt.

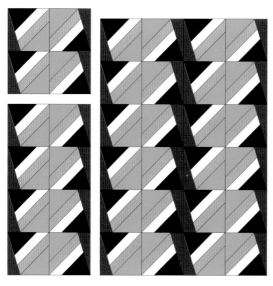

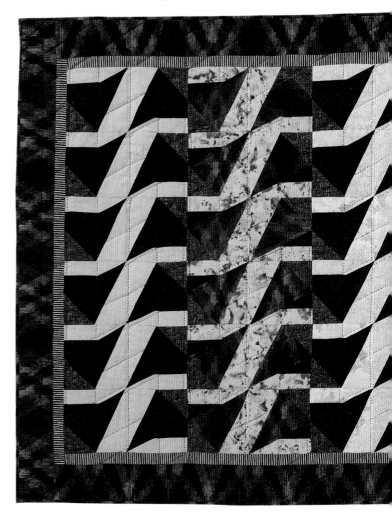

Variation 2:

Place a **row** of rotated blocks underneath a row of basic blocks.

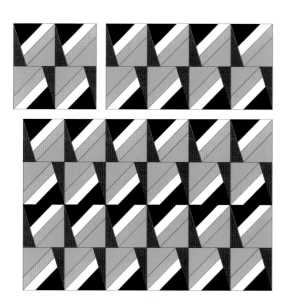

Variation 3:

Alternate the basic block and the rotated block, making sure that row 2 starts with the rotated block not the basic block.

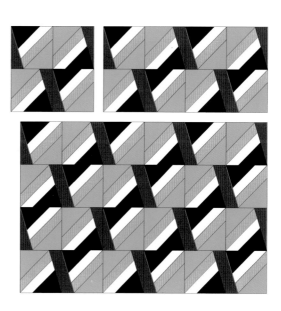

Variation 4:

Make quilts with the illusion of spinning by working with a block and all three rotations of the block i.e. the block is turned through 90°, 180° and 270° in a clockwise direction. *Fireworks,* below and on page 62, is an example of this. Here the 4-block unit starts with the basic block in the top left hand corner.

Variation 5:

Experiment with the starting point of the 4-block unit. What if the basic block was placed in the top right hand corner?

Group 3: Reflection

This group of quilt layouts uses **reflection**.

Variation 1:

Place a column of basic blocks with a column of horizontally reflected blocks beside it.

Variation 3:

Place a column of basic blocks with a column of vertically reflected blocks beside it.

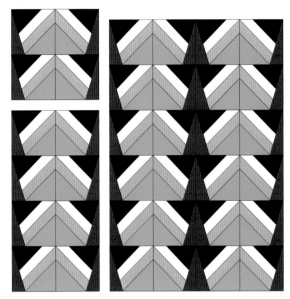

Variation 2:

Place a row of basic blocks with a row of vertically reflected blocks underneath it.

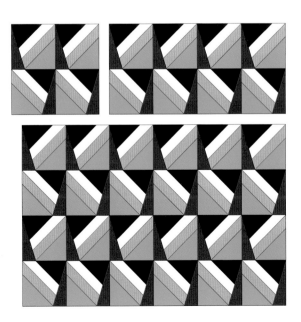

Variation 4:

Place a row of basic blocks with a row of horizontally reflected blocks underneath it.

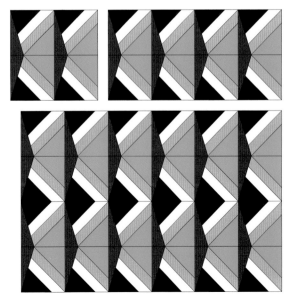

Variation 5:

The basic block is in the top left corner and beside it is its vertical reflection. Underneath these two blocks, the original two have switched places with the basic block on the right and the reflection on the left. Look at *Shadehouse*, right and on page 66, to see how this layout looks.

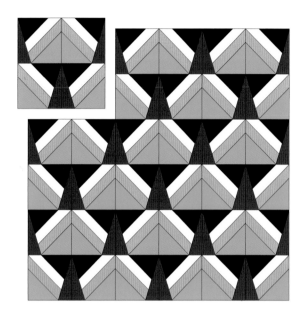

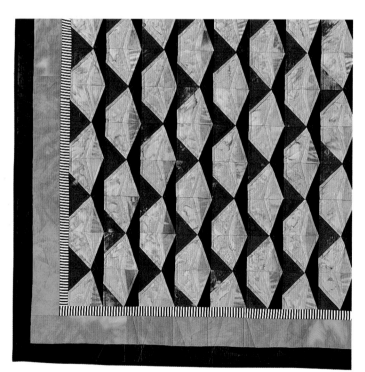

Variation 6:

Here, the basic block remains in the top left corner, but this time its horizontal reflection is placed beside it. Again the blocks have switched places in the row below with the basic block on the right and the reflection on the left. This layout is shown in *Times Four*, left.

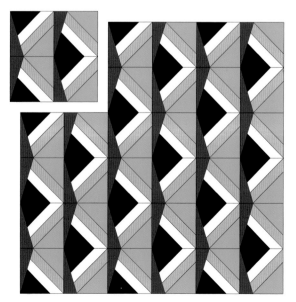

Group 4: Reflection and Rotation

Variation 1:

The basic block is in the upper left corner. Beside it is its horizontal reflection. Immediately below the basic block is a vertical reflection of the basic block and beside that is an 180° rotation of the basic block. *Little Treasure*, below and on page 86, shows how this combination works.

Variation 2:

Here, the basic block is in the upper left corner and beside it is its vertical reflection. Immediately below is a 270° clockwise rotation of the reflected block. Next to it is a 90° clockwise rotation of the basic block.

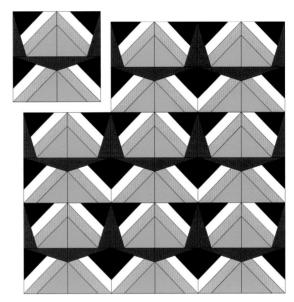

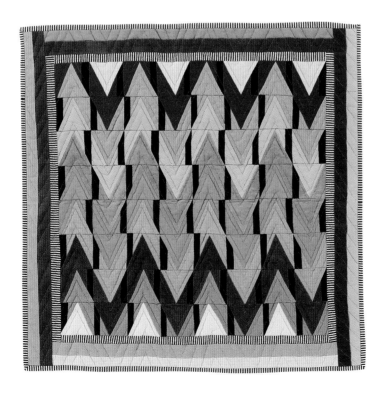

Variation 3:

For this layout, the basic block remains in the upper left corner and beside it is a 180° rotation of it. Below the basic block is its horizontal reflection. Beside that is a 180° rotation of the reflected block. **Waves,** above and on page 71, uses this quilt layout.

Variation 4:

The basic block is placed in the upper left corner. Beside it is its vertical reflection. Immediately below the basic block is its horizontal reflection and beside it is a 180° rotation of the basic block. Look at **Times Four** on page 23.

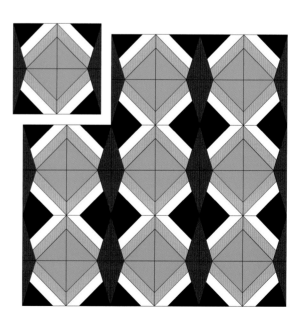

Variation 5:

This time an 8-block unit rather than the 4-block unit in Variations 1 - 4 will be considered. The 8-block unit is comprised of two 4-block units as shown below.

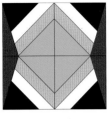
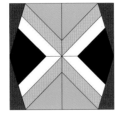

Layout A   Layout B

In Layout A, the basic block is in the upper left corner. Beside it is its vertical reflection. Below the basic block is its horizontal reflection. Next to it is a 180° rotation of the basic block.

In Layout B, the basic block has a new position in the bottom left corner and beside it is its vertical reflection. Above the basic block is its horizontal reflection and beside that is a 180° rotation of the basic block. In fact, the two rows from Layout A have switched places in Layout B. Combining A and B gives an exciting quilt layout.

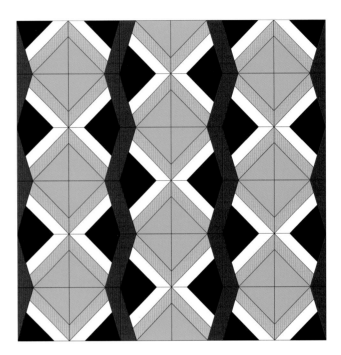

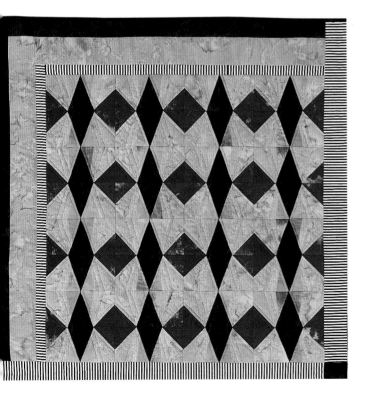

A quadrant of *Times Four*
by Carolyn Sullivan
(not included as a project
in this book) showing
Variation 4 layout

Variation 6:

Here, four of the 4-block units are required to see how the pattern falls into place.

Combination 1:

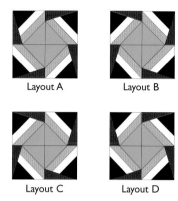

In Layout A, the basic block is in the upper left corner. Beside it the basic block is rotated 90° clockwise. Underneath that the basic block has been rotated 180° clockwise. In the bottom left, the basic block has been rotated 270° clockwise.

In Layout B, the upper left corner is now a vertical reflection of the block in the upper right of Layout A. This is not as complex as it seems because they will sit beside one another when they are placed in the full layout. The other blocks in Layout B are now rotations of that initial block. The upper right is a 90° clockwise rotation of the upper left block, the lower right is an 180° clockwise rotation of the upper left block and the last block, in the lower left, is a 270° clockwise rotation of the upper left block.

Layout C is the same as Layout B, Layout D is the same as Layout A. Combining them creates a stunning quilt layout.

There are three more possible combinations of these rotated and reflected blocks. It is the placement of the basic block that will change them.

Combination 2:

Place the basic block in the top right instead of the top left.

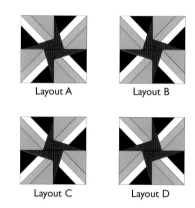

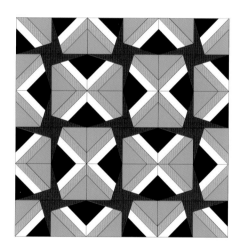

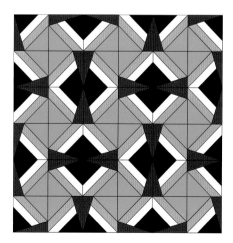

Combination 3:

Place the basic block in the lower left corner.

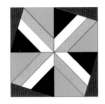

Layout A

Layout B

Layout C

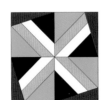

Layout D

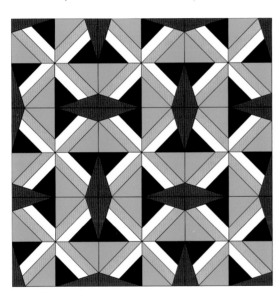

Combination 4:

Place the basic block in the lower right hand corner.

Layout A

Layout B

Layout C

Layout D

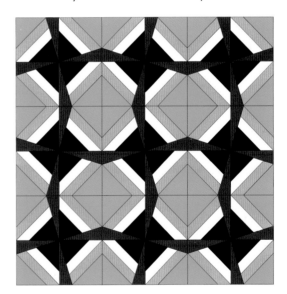

Turning your blocks into quilts

These are the other blocks that have been designed and used to make the quilts in this book.

When all the layout variations are applied to these blocks, a whole gallery of quilts can be designed. At the end of most projects, you will find eight examples of quilt designs and six different layouts in black and white for you to enlarge and color.

These days it is easy to go to a good computer program and learn how to design your own quilts using the functions built into the program. There are a number of these programs on the market and they enable you to draw your own block and then repeat, rotate and reflect it.

However, not everyone has access to these programs, nor the interest. For some quilters, it is much more fun actually making the quilts than spending time learning a computer program. I feel I fit very nicely into this category as I love making quilts and was very reluctant to design quilts using a computer. As time has gone by, and I found so many blocks that I wanted to play with, it became urgent to learn new skills.

To work without a computer, however, requires access to a photocopier. I used to go to my local library and spend hours there cutting and pasting little squares, then photocopying some more. It is best to start with a page of the block you have designed and make a number of photocopies of your page before you begin playing with them.

The most sensible way to make a reflected image of a block is to tape one of the photocopied pages to a window with the back of the page facing you and draw the images onto the back of the page, then photocopy that. You can then apply the suggestions as listed, again using scissors and paste.

Have fun designing new blocks and quilt layouts.

Making Color Decisions

Once you have designed several quilt layouts following the suggestions given, it is important to keep a master copy of each of them. Make a number of photo-copies of the completed quilt layouts and then use coloring pencils or colored felt pens to color them in. There is no way to stress how important it is to color as many as you can so that lots of possibilities can be considered. Of course, the colorings will not be as detailed as actual quilts, as a box of coloring pencils or felt pens only has a limited number of colors. When using quilting fabrics, on the other hand, you will have a much wider variety of colors and patterns. But coloring by hand will enable you to see the secondary patterns that emerge with different colorways.

Compare the coloring of the three layouts below. In the non-colored version of the block, it is difficult to 'see' the pattern because there are so many lines and there is no color definition. When it is shaded with every block the same color, the design has clarity and becomes more appealing. However, there are much more interesting things to do with the design. When the colors zigzag in lines across the quilt layout, the result is a much more dynamic quilt. This is a modified version of *Little Treasure* on page 86.

Black and white designs are included at the end of each project. Enlarge and photocopy these designs to experiment with lots of different colorings to help make fabulous quilts using your own color ideas. They are provided for personal use only.

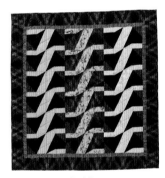
Red Ikat

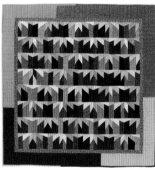
Shadehouse

Some personal thoughts on color

Color is an essential part of any quilt and is very personal. It may be subdued, muted color or vibrant, shocking color. Both are effective uses of color. Compare the softer colors in **Red Ikat** with the much bolder colors in **Shadehouse**, above. The patterns in **Shadehouse** are very small and angular and in order to make them stand out, the color needs to be strong. Yet, in **Red Ikat**, the pieces are not so intricate, and a more subdued palette can be used.

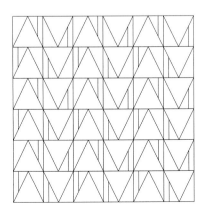

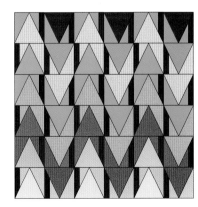

Value of color

The rules relating to the color wheel can be quite detailed and, while it is important to have some understanding of these basic rules, there are other aspects of color theory that have been more important to me. The **value** of a color is the aspect of color theory that has been most important to me and is the one that I use most often. Value is the relative darkness or lightness of a color.

| A | B | C |

Here are three color variations of the same block. A is far too dark and would make a very dark, sombre quilt. To make a very dark quilt work, include some highlights of light fabrics somewhere in the quilt. B is very light. Quilts made in these soft shades need some relief from the softness to give them depth. C gives the most variation in tonal value and is likely to be the most interesting quilt.

| A | B |

In A, there is a strong contrast between light and dark. There is less of a contrast between the dark and light colors in B. There is a place for both ideas in your quilts.

Intensity of color

The intensity of a color also matters. Intensity is the strength of a color; how clear the color is and whether it has been dulled by the addition of black or white.

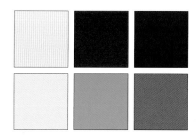

This diagram is an example of intensity. The pure red is in the centre square with a whitened version

(tint) to the left and a blackened version (shade) to the right. Likewise the turquoise at the centre is pure with a tint to the left and a shade to the right.

In *Palm Fronds* (above, top), the yellow and turquoise together are both very intense. They add vibrancy to the quilt. On the other hand, in *Spinning in Blue* (above, bottom), there is also a bright turquoise but with a tint of turquoise beside it. This light turquoise tends to soften the intensity of the bright turquoise and hence the whole quilt.

From this then, it is possible to see that colors can depend for their intensity on the colors that surround them. I particularly like to use the purer versions of the color that have not been dulled by the addition of black and white. This is a personal choice and not one that is favored by everyone.

Sometimes it helps to be a bit intuitive about color selection. In *Underneath the Arches*, page 82, there is a lot of concentrated color all put together in one quilt. It probably breaks many of the conventions of color usage, yet it works because of the strength of the color. For someone who prefers a softer palette, however, the strength of the color would be off-putting.

There are some colors that I like more than others. If you look at the collection of quilts in *Quilted*

One Block Marvels, you will see that almost every quilt has red in it. Red is such a versatile color and adds a warm touch to a quilt. Also, I particularly like yellow, purple and turquoise. You will notice that there is a lot of yellow in the quilts too. It can be an intense yellow as in *Palm Fronds* or a more subdued yellow as in *Fireworks*. I very rarely use brown. Because I love color so much, I see brown as a very drab color. Yet it can be used very effectively in combination with other colors. I have used it with an earthy red, navy and turquoise and created very pleasing results.

All of these quilts rely on the strong pattern of the designs and, in order to have those patterns predominate, color needs to enhance them. This is why quite often in the quilts in this book you will notice that I have selected one color for use in the same piece in each template. In *In Flight*, the navy always comes in the same position in the block, as does the pink, the light blue and the yellow. In order for the quilt to be more interesting, I often select more than one fabric in a color choice. Rather than use one navy fabric, I will use a number of navy fabrics. That way, I am using the texture of the print to assist in making the quilt more exciting. The materials list for the projects often suggests that a variety of prints in one color be used.

I am often asked how I get my ideas for color. When you are looking at the world around you, take time to observe and look for color ideas. How many variations of blue do you see in the sky during the day? What other colors can you see in the sky, particularly at sunrise and sunset?

What colors are the houses? What colors are used on billboards? Visit places where there is lots of color. What about the gardens in your community? You can get wonderful color choices from a garden. Visit your local hardware store and get some of the house paint color swatches. Look in magazines and see what colors are used in the advertising, house decoration, paintings, food and so on. Collect your ideas in a scrapbook.

You do not have to go far from home to see lots of color. The bowl of fruit and vegetables picked from my garden shows a variety of color from the red and green of the chillies, the orange of the tomatoes and the deep purple of the passionfruit.

The beautiful mauve of the jacaranda tree makes a heart-warming display each November.

And the superb colors of the sunset always create a dramatic atmosphere and give wonderful ideas for color combinations. Like good design, color choices are everywhere – you just need to look. So remember to look at your world and think about it in a new way!

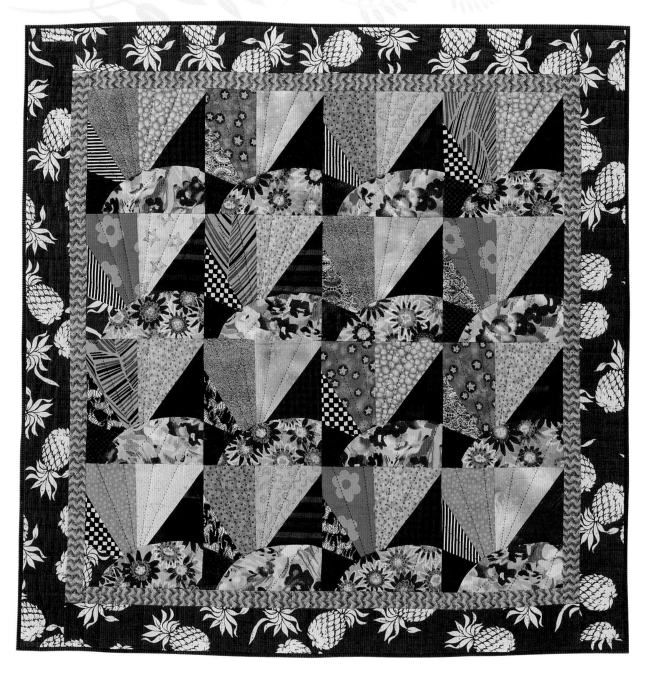

Palm Fronds
Finished size: 42in x 42in (108cm x 108cm)
Block size: 8in (20cm)

Palm Fronds

 This quilt uses simple **repetition** of the **Palm Fronds** block, which was inspired by a photograph of palm fronds. The radiating leaves of the plant lend themselves to lovely shapes and the addition of a curve in the block makes the design more sinuous.

MATERIALS

½yd (40cm) in total of a variety of red fabrics (Template A)

½yd (40cm) in total of a variety of yellow fabrics (Template B)

½yd (40cm) in total of a variety of turquoise fabrics (Template C)

½yd (40cm) in total of a variety of black and white fabrics (Template D)

½yd (40cm) in total of a variety of dark blue fabrics (Template E)

½yd (40cm) of one or more boldly patterned fabrics (Template F). In Palm Fronds as shown, two different fabrics are used.

¼yd (25cm) black and white fabric (Border 1)

¾yd (70cm) large print fabric (Border 2)

½yd (40cm) red striped fabric (binding)

3yd (2.8m) backing fabric

Batting at least 52in x 52in (128cm x 128cm)

Tracing paper

Flower pins

Neutral thread

Perle No.12 thread in a shade to match (optional for hand quilting)

Chenille needle (optional for hand quilting with Perle thread)

CUT THE FABRIC

Note:

i) Templates are on page 34. Detailed instructions are given for Preparing the Templates and Using Templates in Techniques for Quiltmaking on page 92. Remember the templates provided do **not** include seam allowances.

ii) Although instructions are given for cutting out the whole quilt, it is preferable to cut out and make up one block first to confirm the accuracy of your piecing.

From the red fabrics, cut:
• 16 Template A. Mark the notch on the curved seam. Remember to place the template **right side up** on the **right side** of the fabric, securing with flower pins. Lay the ruler with the ¼in line against one side of the template and cut along the ruler. Repeat for all sides of the template except the curved seam. For the curved seam, estimate the ¼in seam allowance by eye and cut out with scissors.

From the yellow fabrics, cut:
• 16 Template B

From the turquoise fabrics, cut:
• 16 Template C

From the black and white fabrics, cut:
• 16 Template D

From the dark blue fabrics, cut:
• 16 Template E. Mark the notch on the curved seam.

From the boldly patterned fabrics, cut:
• 16 Template F. Mark the notches on the curved edge.

From the black and white fabric for Border 1, cut:
• 4 strips, 1¾in x width of fabric

From the large print fabric for Border 2, cut:
• 5 strips, 4in x width of fabric. Join the strips end to end.

From the red striped fabric, cut:
• 5 strips, 2½in x width of fabric for the binding.

MAKE THE BLOCKS

1. Sew A to B. Press the seam towards A.

2. Sew C to D. Press the seam towards C.

3. Sew these two sections together, pressing the seam towards B.

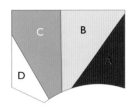

4. Sew E to D. Press seam towards D.

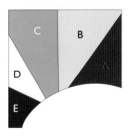

5. Pin the curved edge in F, matching the notches to the notches in A and E to ensure accuracy. Stitch in place pressing the seam away from F. Make 16 blocks.

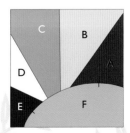

ASSEMBLE THE QUILT

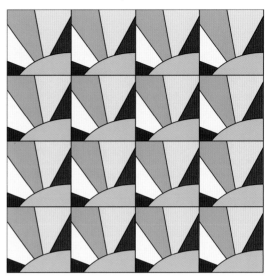

Quilt center

1. Lay the blocks out in rows across the quilt making sure their orientation is correct.

Row 1 – basic block repeated four times.

Repeat this row four times.

2. Join the blocks into rows. Press the seams of each row in the opposite direction to the previous row so that the seams can be butted when the rows are joined.

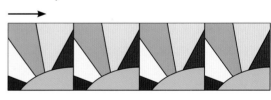

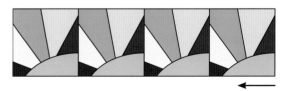

3. To complete the quilt center, join the rows, butting the seams and making sure all points and joins match.

ADD THE BORDERS

1. Referring to Adding Borders with Square Corners in Techniques for Quiltmaking on page 94, measure the width of the quilt across the center of the quilt. Trim two 1¾in strips of black and white print to that length.

2. Pin, then sew a strip to the top and bottom edge of the quilt, matching centers. Press the seam allowances towards the borders.

3. In the same manner, measure the length of the quilt through the center of the quilt. Trim two 1¾in strips of black and white fabric to that length.

4. Pin, then sew a strip to the left and right edges of the quilt, matching centers. Press the seam allowances towards the borders.

5. Repeat steps 1-4 with the 4in strips of large print fabric, joining strips where necessary.

FINISH THE QUILT

1. Cut the length of backing fabric in half. Remove the selvages. Join the two sections together lengthwise, then trim to 54in square for the quilt backing.

2. Layer the backing, batting and quilt top. Pin or thread baste all the layers together.

3. Quilt as desired, either by machine or hand. *Palm Fronds* as shown was hand quilted with black Perle No.12 thread with lines radiating away from the curved seam line. This quilting pattern replicates more of the lines of the palm fronds from the original source of inspiration. When hand quilting with Perle No.12 thread, use a small chenille needle rather than a quilting needle because it is much stronger.

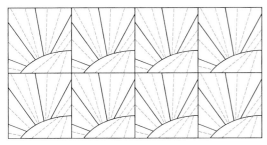

Quilting design for *Palm Fronds*

4. Bind the quilt with the 2½in strips of red striped fabric, referring to Binding the Quilt in Techniques for Quiltmaking on page 95. Label your quilt.

Comment on Color

The very rich, green growth seen in the inspirational photograph of palm fronds suggested the use of fabrics to give a bright, tropical feel. The colors are all crisp, bold and evocative, reminiscent of an island in the sun. Blue and turquoise together with yellow are very intense and the blue pineapple fabric on the border completes the impression of a hot, steamy climate.

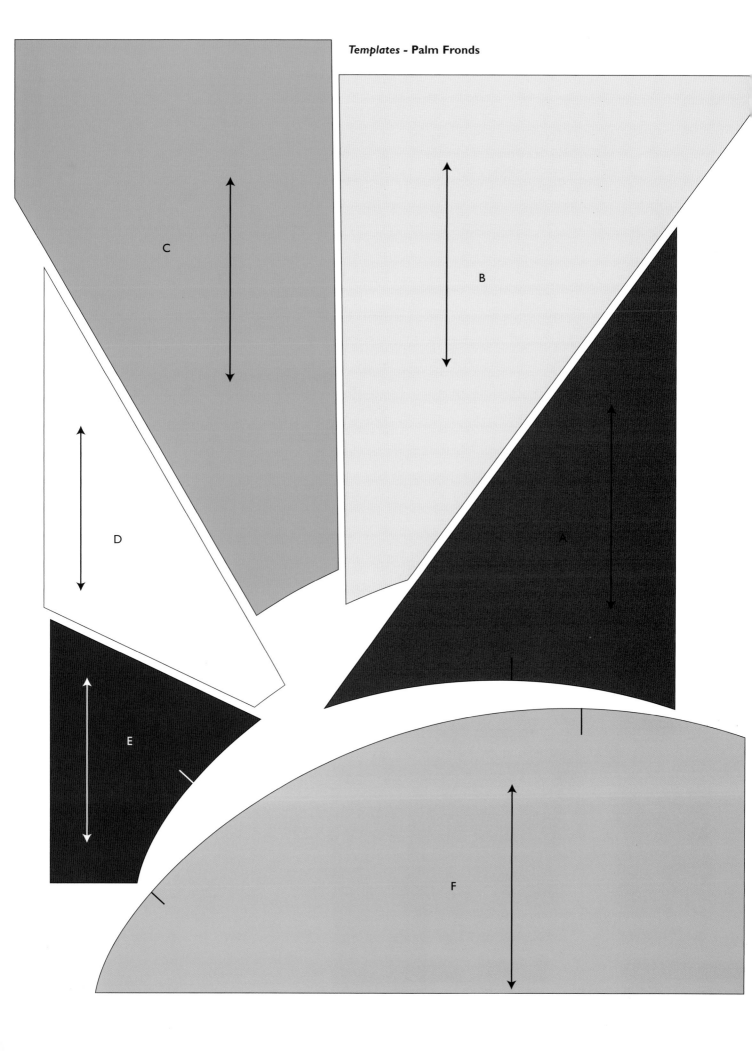

Templates - Palm Fronds

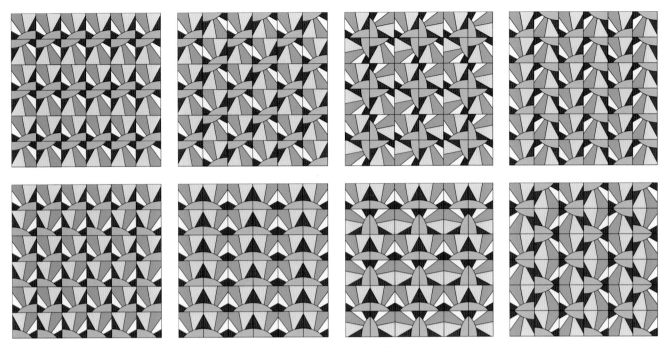

Alternative layouts for the **Palm Fronds** block.

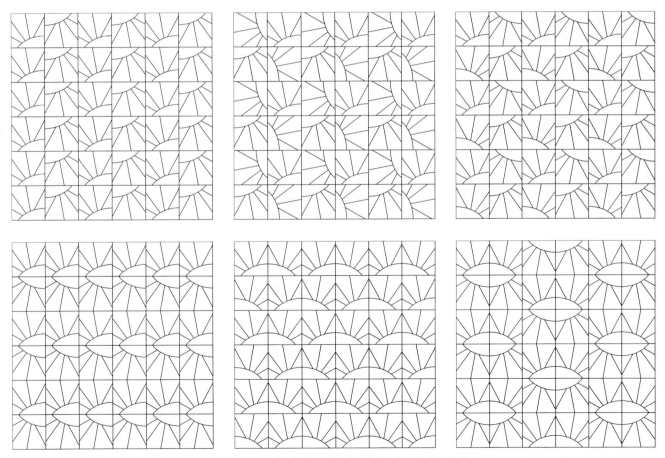

Enlarge and color to create new quilt designs for the **Palm Fronds** block. For personal use only.

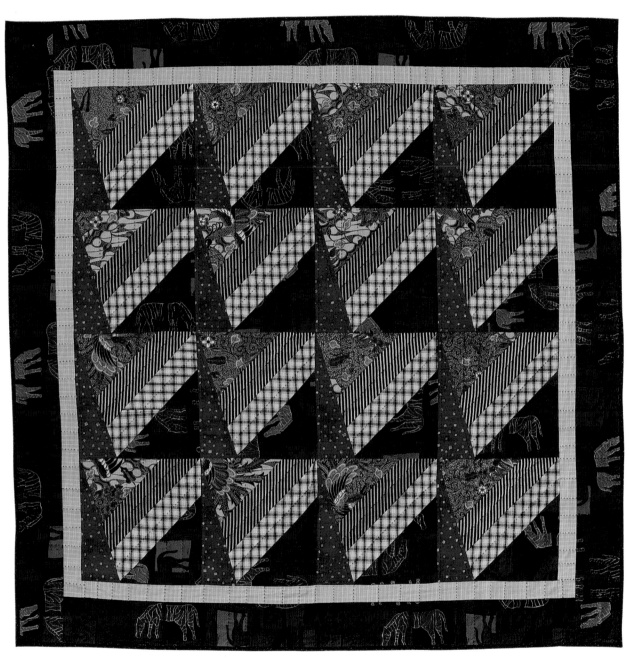

On Safari
Finished size: 42in x 42in (107cm x 107cm)
Block size: 8in (20cm)

On Safari

 *This quilt uses simple **repetition** of the block. The **On Safari** block is a combination of ideas from blocks inspired by the Sydney Olympic Stadium and has been used extensively in Chapter 2, Turning Blocks into Quilts starting on page 12.*

MATERIALS

1¼yd (1m) African fabric (Template A and Border 2)

½yd (40cm) checked fabric (Template B)

½yd (40cm) striped fabric (Template C)

½yd (40cm) batik fabric (Template D)

½yd (40cm) red fabric (Template E)

¼yd (25cm) mauve fabric (Border 1)

½yd (40cm) purple fabric (binding)

3yd (2.8m) backing fabric

Batting at least 53in x 53in (135cm x 135cm)

Tracing paper

Flower pins

Neutral thread

Perle No.12 thread in a shade to match (optional for hand quilting)

Chenille needle (optional for hand quilting with Perle thread)

CUT THE FABRIC

Note:

*i) Templates are on page 40. Detailed instructions are given for Preparing Templates and Using Templates in Techniques for Quiltmaking on page 92. Remember the templates provided do **not** include a seam allowance.*

ii) Although instructions are given for cutting out the whole quilt, it is preferable to cut out and make up one block first to confirm the accuracy of your piecing

From the African fabric, cut:

- *5 strips, 4in x width of fabric (Border 2)*
- *16 Template A. Remember to place the template **right side up** on the **right side** of the fabric, securing with flower pins. Lay the ruler with the ¼in line against one side of the template and cut along the ruler. Repeat for all sides of the template.*

From the checked fabric, cut:

- *16 Template B*

From the striped fabric, cut:

- *16 Template C*

From the batik fabric, cut:

- *16 Template D*

From the red fabric, cut:

- *16 Template E*

From the mauve fabric, cut:

- *4 strips, 1¾in x width of fabric (Border 1)*

From the purple fabric, cut:

- *5 strips, 2½in x width of fabric (binding)*

MAKE THE BLOCKS

1. Sew A to B. Press the seam towards A.

2. Sew C to D. Press the seam towards C. Sew these two sections together, pressing the seam towards B.

3. Add E. Press the seam towards D to complete the *On Safari* block. Make 16.

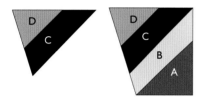

ASSEMBLE THE QUILT

Quilt center

1. Lay the blocks out in rows across the quilt making sure their orientation is correct.

Row 1 – basic block repeated four times.

Repeat this row four times.

2. Join the blocks into rows. Press the seams of each row in the opposite direction to the previous row so that the seams can be butted when the rows are joined.

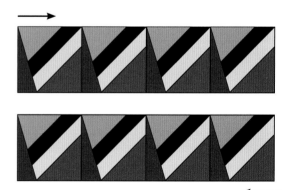

3. To complete the quilt center, join the rows, butting the seams and making sure all points and joins match.

ADD THE BORDERS

1. Referring to Adding Borders with Square Corners in Techniques for Quiltmaking on page 94, measure the width of the quilt across the center of the quilt. Trim two 1¾in strips of mauve fabric to that length.

2. Pin, then sew a strip to the top and bottom edges of the quilt, matching centers. Press the seam allowances towards the borders.

3. In the same manner, measure the length of the quilt through the center. Trim two 1¾in strips of mauve fabric to that length.

4. Pin, then sew a strip to the right and left edges of the quilt, matching centers. Press the seam allowances towards the borders.

5. Repeat steps 1-4 with the 4in strips of African fabric, joining strips where necessary for Border 2.

FINISH THE QUILT

1. Cut the length of backing fabric in half. Remove the selvages. Join the two sections together lengthwise, then trim to 54in square for the quilt backing.

2. Layer the backing, batting and quilt top. Pin or thread-baste all the layers together.

3. Quilt as desired, either by machine or hand. *On Safari* was hand quilted using Perle No.12 thread. The quilting outlines the red triangle then radiates lines away from the triangle through pieces B, C and D. When hand quilting with No.12 Perle thread use a small chenille needle rather than a quilting needle because it is much stronger.

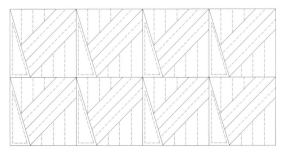

Quilting design for *On Safari*

4. Bind the quilt with the 2½in strips of purple fabric referring to Binding the Quilt in Techniques for Quiltmaking on page 95. Label the quilt.

Comment on Color

*I**n On Safari**, a favorite African fabric dictated the color choices for the remaining fabrics. The main colors in the African fabric are brown, red and purple, so selecting these colors made for a very successful palette for the quilt. This is often the easiest way to create a great color scheme for your quilt. A very bright red was chosen because of its boldness and dramatic effect in the quilt. And rather than just making color decisions for the other fabrics, fabrics with different kinds of printed designs were selected including a stripe, a batik and a check that all worked well with the African fabric.*

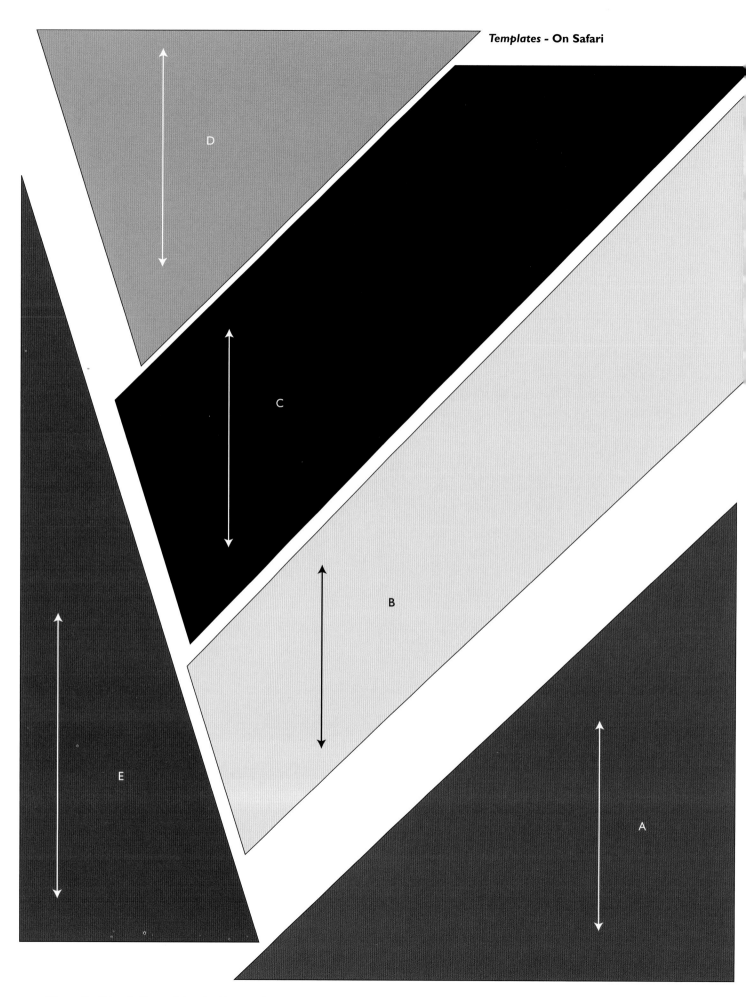

D

C

B

A

E

Enlarge and color to create new quilt designs for **On Safari** and **In The Temple** blocks. For personal use only.

In the Temple
Finished size: 47in x 47in (119 x 119cm)
Block size: 6in (15cm)

In the Temple

In the Temple block

Horizontal reflection of *In the Temple* block

In the Temple uses the same block design as **On Safari** but the block is smaller and is used with the **horizontal reflection** of the basic block to give a totally different arrangement.

MATERIALS

½yd (40cm) of a Japanese fan fabric (Template A, Ar)

½yd (40cm) in total of a variety of ochre fabrics including stripes (Template B, Br)

½yd (40cm) in total of a variety of black and gold textured fabrics (Template C, Cr)

½yd (40cm) of a black and white batik (Template D, Dr)

½yd (40cm) in total of a variety of red fabrics (Template E, Er)

¼yd (25cm) purple tone-on-tone fabric (Border 1)

½yd (40cm) of peach tone-on-tone fabric (Border 2)

¾yd (80cm) brown and black batik (Border 3)

½yd (40cm) mustard fabric (binding)

3yd (2.8m) backing fabric

Batting at least 55in x 55in (139cm x 139cm)

Tracing paper

Flower pins

Neutral thread

Quilting thread (black)

CUT THE FABRIC

Note:

i) Templates are on page 46. Detailed instructions are given for Preparing Templates and Using Templates in Techniques for Quiltmaking on page 92. Remember the templates provided do **not** include seam allowances.

ii) Although instructions are given for cutting out the whole quilt, it is preferable to cut out and make up one block first to confirm the accuracy of your piecing.

From the Japanese fan print, cut:

• 15 Template A. Remember to place the template **right side up** on the **right side** of the fabric, securing with flower pins. Lay the ruler with the ¼in line against one side of the template and cut along the ruler. Repeat for all sides of the template.

• 10 Template Ar

From the ochre fabrics, cut

• 15 Template B
• 10 Template Br

From the black and gold fabrics, cut:

• 15 Template C
• 10 Template Cr

From the black and white batik, cut:

• 15 Template D
• 10 Template Dr

From the red fabrics, cut:

• 15 Template E
• 10 Template Er

From the purple fabric, cut:

• 4 strips, 1¾in x width of fabric (Border 1)

From the peach tone-on-tone fabric, cut:

• 4 strips, 3in x width of fabric (Border 2)

From the black and brown batik, cut:

• 5 strips, 5in x width of fabric (Border 3)

From the mustard fabric, cut:

• 5 strips, 2½in x width of fabric (binding).

MAKE THE BLOCKS

For *In the Temple*, there are 15 basic blocks using Templates A-E and 10 reflected blocks using Templates Ar-Er

1. Sew A to B for the basic block and Ar to Br for the reflected block. Press the seam towards A and Ar.

2. Sew C to D and Cr to Dr. Press the seam towards C and Cr.

3. Sew A/B to C/D and Ar/Br to Cr/Dr. Press the seam towards B and Br.

4. Sew E and Er in place. Press the seam towards E and Er.

Make 15 basic blocks and 10 reflected blocks.

ASSEMBLE THE QUILT

Quilt center

1. Lay the blocks out in rows across the quilt making sure their orientation is correct.

Row 1 – five basic blocks.

Row 2 – five horizontally reflected blocks.

These two rows are repeated down the quilt once then Row 1 is repeated again.

2. Join the blocks into rows. Press the seams of each row in the opposite direction to the previous row so that the seams can be butted when they are joined.

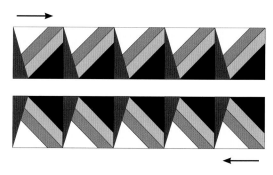

3. To complete the quilt center, join the rows, butting the seams and making sure all points and joins match.

ADD THE BORDERS

1. Referring to Adding Borders with Square Corners in Techniques for Quiltmaking on page 94, measure the width of the quilt across the center of the quilt. Trim two 1¾in strips of purple fabric to that length.

2. Pin, then sew a strip to the top and bottom edges of the quilt, matching centers. Press the seam allowances towards the borders.

3. In the same manner, measure the length of the quilt through the center of the quilt. Trim two 1¾in strips of purple fabric to that length.

4. Pin, then sew a strip to the right and left edges of the quilt, matching centers. Press the seam allowances towards the borders.

5. Repeat steps 1-4 with the 3in strips of peach tone-on-tone fabric for Border 2 and the 5in strips of black and brown batik fabric for Border 3, joining strips as required.

FINISH THE QUILT

1. Cut the length of backing fabric in half. Remove the selvages. Join the two sections lengthwise, then trim to 55in square for the backing of the quilt.

2. Layer the backing, batting and quilt top. Pin or thread-baste all the layers together.

3. Quilt as desired, either by machine or hand. *In the Temple* was hand quilted using quilting thread. The peach border was quilted with parallel lines and the design on the batik has been outlined on Border 3.

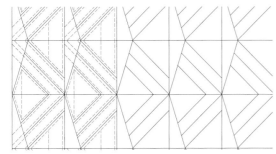

Quilting design for *In the Temple*

4. Bind the quilt with the 2½in strips of mustard fabric referring to Binding the Quilt in Techniques for Quiltmaking on page 95. Label your quilt.

Note: For new quilt designs for the *In the Temple* block, see page 41.

Comment on Color

In the Temple *is a great name for a quilt that combines several fabrics that feature designs based on different cultures. Combining these fabrics creates a richness that only traditional design can achieve. The black and white Indonesian batik provides an interesting contrast to the collection of vibrant red and ochre fabrics, which emphasise the design.*

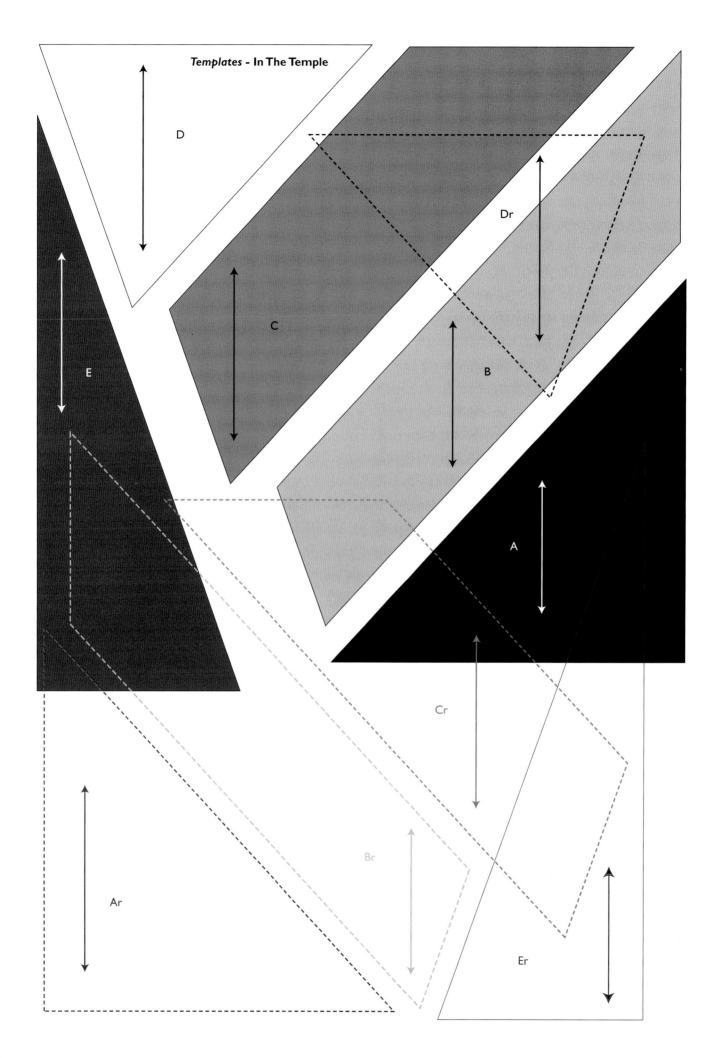

Templates - **In The Temple**

D

Dr

C

B

E

A

Cr

Br

Ar

Er

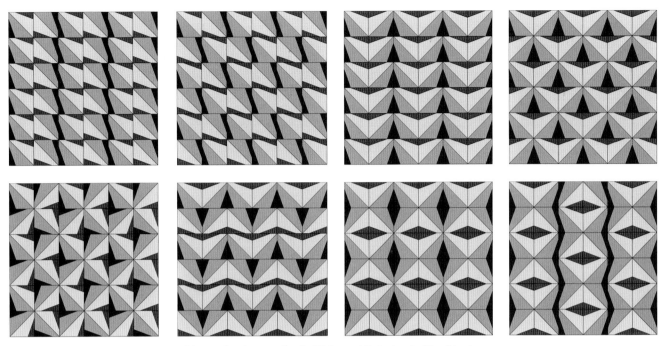

Alternative layouts for *In Flight* and *Spinning In Blue* blocks

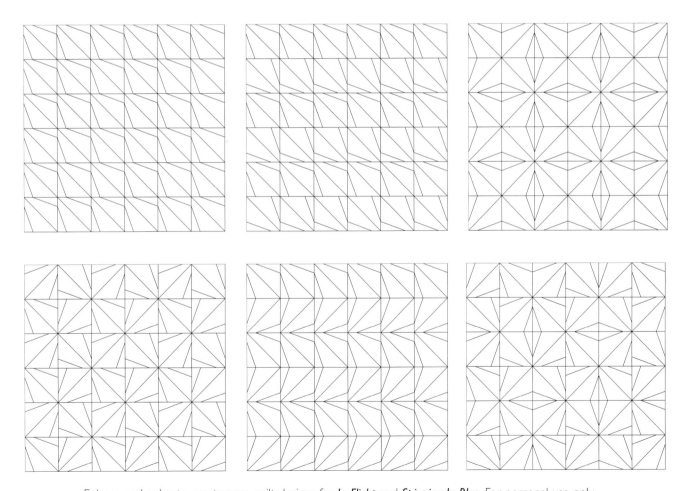

Enlarge and color to create new quilt designs for *In Flight* and *Spinning In Blue*. For personal use only.

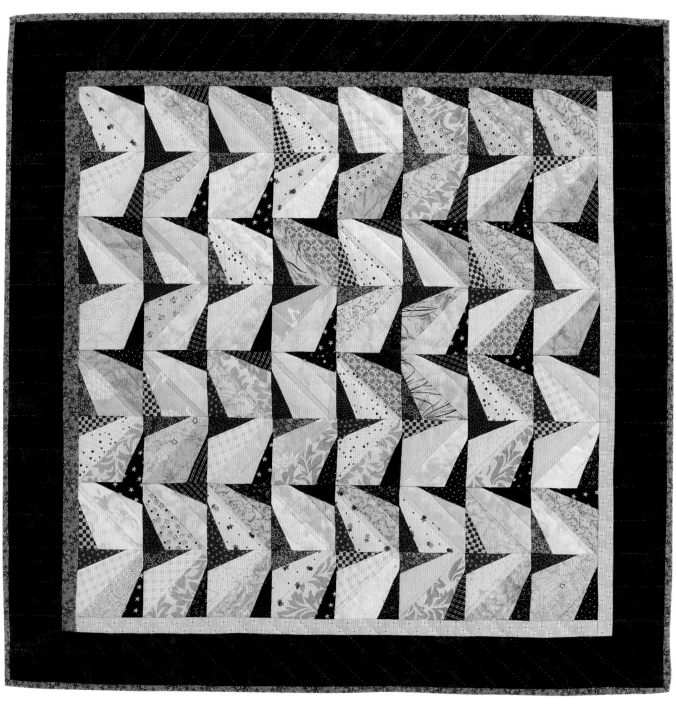

In Flight

Finished size: 31in x 31in (79cm x 79cm)

Block size: 3in (7.5cm)

In Flight

*In Flight uses **rotation** of the block in its design. The basic block forms the first row, and then the block is rotated 90° for the second row. This design creates a lovely mood of flight with the navy and pink birds flying in opposite directions.*

 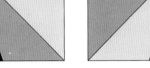

In Flight block   *In Flight* block
rotated 90°

MATERIALS

³⁄₈ yd (30cm) in total of a variety of pink
    fabrics

³⁄₈ yd (30cm) in total of a variety of yellow
    fabrics

³⁄₈ yd (30cm) in total of a variety of light blue
    fabrics

³⁄₈ yd (30cm) in total of a variety of navy
    fabrics

¹⁄₈ yd (10cm) extra yellow fabric (Border 1)

¹⁄₂ yd (40cm) extra light blue fabric (Border 1
    and binding)

¹⁄₂ yd (40cm) extra navy fabric (Border 2)

1¹⁄₄ yd (1m) backing fabric

Batting at least 39in x 39in (99cm x 99cm)

⁷⁄₈ yd (70cm) light weight no iron interfacing

Dressmakers' carbon

Tracing paper

Flower pins

Ballpoint pen

Neutral thread for piecing and hand quilting

CUT THE FABRIC

From the extra yellow fabric, cut:
- *2 strips, 1¼in x width of fabric (Border 1)*

From the extra light blue fabric, cut:
- *2 strips, 1¼in x width of fabric (Border 1)*
- *4 strips, 2½in x width of fabric (binding).*

From the extra navy fabric, cut;
- *4 strips, 3¼in x width of fabric (Border 2)*

MAKE THE BLOCKS

1. Referring to Making Blocks with Foundations in Techniques for Quiltmaking, page 93, prepare foundations for 64 blocks using the *In Flight* Foundation Diagram below.

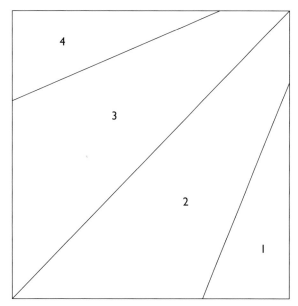

Foundation for *In Flight*

2. Remember when working on foundations that it is best to overestimate the size of the fabric required for each shape, then trim away the excess after stitching. Remember to sew on the **wrong** (marked) side of the foundation with the fabric pieces on the right (unmarked) side of the foundation.

3. Pin shape 1 in pink with its wrong side to the right (unmarked) side of the foundation. See Step 1 in Making Blocks with Foundations, page 93.

4. Pin shape 2 in yellow with its right side facing the right side of shape 1. Turn the foundation over. Stitch along the seam line between shapes 1 and 2 on the foundation, extending the stitching into the seam allowance at the start and finish of the seam. Turn the foundation back. Trim away any excess seam allowance. Push shape 2 back over the seam, finger press and pin it in place. See Step 2 in Making Blocks with Foundations, page 93.

5. Sew shape 3 in light blue to the foundation in the same way. See Step 3 in Making Blocks with Foundations, page 93.

6. Sew shape 4 in navy to the foundation in the same way. Make 64 blocks.

ASSEMBLE THE QUILT

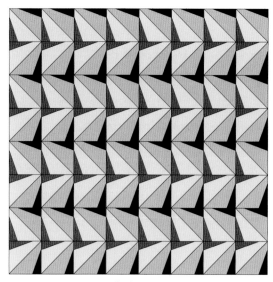

Quilt center

1. Lay the blocks out in rows across the quilt, making sure their orientation is correct.

Row 1 – basic block repeated eight times.

Row 2 – basic block rotated 90° clockwise repeated eight times.

Repeat these two rows four times.

2. Join the blocks into rows. Press the seams of each row in the opposite direction to the previous row so that the seams can be butted when the rows are joined.

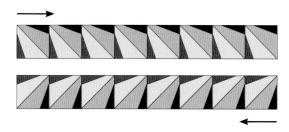

3. To complete the quilt center, join the rows, butting the seams and making sure all points and joins match.

ADD THE BORDERS

1. Referring to Adding Borders with Square Corners in Techniques for Quiltmaking on page 94, measure the width of the quilt across the center. Trim one 1¼in strip of yellow fabric and one 1¼in strip of light blue fabric to that length.

2. Pin, then sew a blue strip to the top edge and a yellow strip to the bottom edge of the quilt, matching centers. Press the seam allowance towards the borders.

3. In the same manner, measure the length of the quilt through the center. Trim one 1¼in strip of yellow fabric and one 1¼in strip of light blue fabric to that length.

4. Pin, then sew a yellow strip to the right edge of the quilt and a blue strip to the left edge of the quilt, matching centers. Press the seam allowance towards the border.

5. Repeat steps 1-4 with the 3¼in strips of extra navy fabric for Border 2.

FINISH THE QUILT

1. Remove the selvages from the backing fabric. Trim to 39in square for the backing of the quilt.

2. Layer the backing, batting and quilt top. Pin or thread baste all the layers together.

3. Quilt as desired, either by machine or hand. *In Flight* was hand quilted in a simple zigzag across the quilt with vertical lines on the top and bottom borders.

Quilting design for *In Flight*

4. Bind the quilt with the 2½in strips of light blue fabric, referring to Binding the Quilt in Techniques for Quiltmaking on page 95. Label your quilt.

Comment on Color

With such a simple block, it seemed sensible to limit the range of colors. Because there are only four pieces in the block and such a distinctive pattern, it is important to select fabrics that will contrast with each other and highlight the pattern. The strong pink and navy fabrics used here contrast well with one another to create the illusion of flight across the quilt. To strengthen the interlocking triangles of the pattern, choose softer colors like yellow and light blue. These colors provide a suitable backdrop for the 'birds'.

Spinning in Blue
Finished size: *31in x 31in (79cm x 79cm)*
Block size: *3in (7.5cm)*

Spinning in Blue

This design uses a combination of **repetition** and **rotation**.
Multiple blocks of the repeat pattern are rotated around a central point.

Spinning in Blue block

Spinning in Blue
block rotated 90°

Spinning in Blue
block rotated 180°

Spinning in Blue
block rotated 270°

MATERIALS

³⁄₈ yd (30cm) in total of a variety of orange
    fabrics

³⁄₈ yd (30cm) in total of a variety of beige
    fabrics

³⁄₈ yd (30cm) in total of a variety of light
    turquoise fabrics

³⁄₈ yd (30cm) in total of a variety of deep
    turquoise fabrics

¼ yd (25cm) extra beige fabric (Border 1)

½ yd (50cm) extra deep turquoise fabric
    (Border 2 and binding). Note that two
    fabrics were used in Spinning in Blue

1¼ yd (1m) backing fabric

Batting at least 39in x 39in (99cm x 99cm)

⁷⁄₈ yd (70cm) light weight no iron interfacing

Dressmakers' carbon

Tracing paper

Flower pins

Ballpoint pen

Neutral thread for piecing and quilting

CUT THE FABRIC

From the extra beige fabric, cut:

• 4 strips, 1¼in x width of fabric (Border 1)

From the extra deep turquoise fabric, cut:

• 4 strips, 3¼in x width of fabric (Border 2)
• 4 strips, 2½in x width of fabric (binding)

MAKE THE BLOCKS

1. Referring to Making the Blocks with Foundations in Techniques for Quiltmaking, page 93, prepare foundations for 64 blocks using the *Spinning in Blue* Foundation Diagram below.

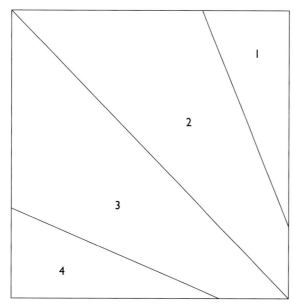

Foundation for *Spinning in Blue*

2. Remember when working on foundations that it is best to overestimate the size of the fabric required for each shape, then trim away the excess after stitching. Remember to sew on the **wrong** (marked) side of the foundation with the fabric pieces on the right (unmarked) side of the foundation.

3. Pin shape 1 in deep turquoise with its wrong side to the right (unmarked) side of the foundation. See Step 1 in Making Blocks with Foundations, page 93.

4. Pin shape 2 in light turquoise with its right side facing the right side of shape 1. Turn the foundation over. Stitch along the seam line between shapes 1 and 2 on the foundation, extending the stitching into the seam allowance at the start and finish of the seam. Turn the foundation back. Trim away any excess seam allowance. Push shape 2 back over the seam, finger press and pin it in place. See Step 2 in Making Blocks with Foundations, page 93.

5. Sew shape 3 in beige to the foundation in the same way. See Step 3 in Making Blocks with Foundations, page 93.

6. Sew shape 4 in orange to the foundation in the same way. Make 64 blocks.

ASSEMBLE THE QUILT

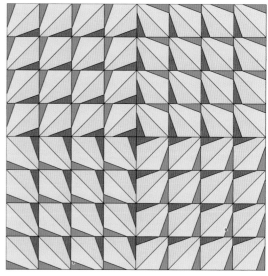

Quilt center

1. Lay the blocks out in rows across the quilt, making sure their orientation is correct.

Rows 1-4 – four basic blocks + four blocks rotated 90° clockwise.

Rows 5-8 – four blocks rotated 270° + four blocks rotated 180°.

2. Join the blocks into rows. Press the seams of each row in the opposite direction to the previous row so the seams can be butted when the rows are joined.

Row 1 – Make 4

Row 5 – Make 4

3. To complete the quilt center, join the rows, butting the seams and making sure all points and joins match.

ADD THE BORDERS

1. Referring to Adding Borders with Square Corners in Techniques for Quiltmaking on page 94, measure the width of the quilt across the center. Trim two 1¼in strips of beige fabric to that length.

2. Pin, then sew a beige strip to the top and bottom edges of the quilt, matching centers. Press the seam allowances towards the borders.

3. In the same manner, measure the length of the quilt through the center. Trim two 1¼in strips of beige fabric to that length.

4. Pin, then sew a beige strip to the left and right edges of the quilt, matching centers. Press the seam allowances towards the borders.

5. Repeat steps 1-4 with the 3¼in strips of deep turquoise fabric for Border 2.

Comment on Color

Turquoise is a beautiful color that can enhance any quilt. Every color seems to work with turquoise. In **Spinning in Blue**, adding lighter shades of turquoise and beige have softened the intensity of the vibrant orange. Beige operates as a neutral color, like grey, and it works very well with other stronger colors. It is useful when you want to color each piece of the block differently to create interest but do not want to have too many colors working against one another. With blocks like these, it is always important to use the colors to enhance the patterns created when the blocks are joined.

FINISH THE QUILT

1. Remove the selvages from the backing fabric. Trim to 39in square for the backing of the quilt.

2. Layer the backing, batting and quilt top. Pin or thread baste all the layers together.

3. Quilt as desired, either by machine or hand. *Spinning in Blue* was machine quilted with concentric squares to enhance and emphasise the design of the quilt.

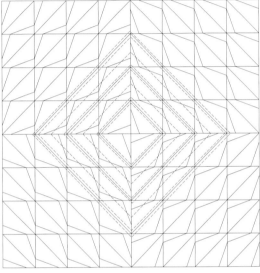

Quilting Design for *Spinning in Blue*

4. Bind the quilt with 2½in strips of deep turquoise, referring to Binding the Quilt in Techniques for Quiltmaking, page 95. Label your quilt.

For alternative color layouts for **Spinning in Blue**, see page 47.

For new quilt designs for you to enlarge and color, see page 47.

The Floral Quilt
Finished size: 89in x 89in (226 x 226cm)
Block size: 4in (10cm)

The Floral Quilt

 *Everyone loves floral quilts and this large quilt made to fit a queen-size bed is no exception. The quilt uses simple **repetition** of the block with the large borders giving the quilt the appearance of a medallion quilt.*

MATERIALS

2yd (2m) in total of a wide variety of floral fabrics (blocks)

½yd (50cm) each of up to eight tone-on-tone pastel fabrics (blocks)

2yd (2m) in total of a variety of white tone-on-tone fabrics (blocks)

1yd (1m) extra white tone-on-tone fabric (Borders 2 and 4)

1yd (80cm) yellow floral fabric (Border 1)

1yd (1m) pink striped fabric (Border 3 and binding)

2½yd (2.3m) large lemon floral fabric (Border 4)

8yd (7.2m) backing fabric

Batting at least 98in x 98in (246cm x 246cm)

Tracing paper

Flower pins

White thread (piecing)

CUT THE FABRIC

Note:

*i) The templates are on page 60. Detailed instructions are given for Preparing Templates and Using Templates in Techniques for Quiltmaking on page 92. Remember the templates provided do **not** include a seam allowance.*

ii) Although instructions are given for cutting out the whole quilt, it is preferable to cut out and make up one block first to confirm the accuracy of your piecing.

From the floral prints, cut:

- *169 Template A. Remember to place the template **right side up** on the **right side** of the fabric, securing with flower pins. Lay the ruler with the ¼in line against one side of the template and cut along the ruler. Repeat for all sides of the template.*

From the tone-on-tone pastel prints, noting that each block requires a B, Br and D cut from the same fabric, cut:

- *169 Template B*
- *169 Template Br*
- *169 Template D*

From the white tone-on-tone fabrics, noting that each block requires a C and Cr cut from the same fabric, cut:

- *169 Template C*
- *169 Template Cr*
- *3 strips, 1½in x width of fabric. Join the strips end to end.*

From the extra white tone-on-tone fabric, cut:

- *14 strips, 2in x width of fabric (Border 2 and 4). Join as required.*

From the yellow floral fabric, cut:

- *6 strips, 4½in x width of fabric (Border 1). Join as required.*

From the pink striped fabric, cut:

- *7 strips, 3in x width of fabric (Border 3). Join as required.*
- *9 strips, 2½in x width of fabric (binding).*

From the large lemon floral fabric, cut:

- *9 strips, 9½in x width of fabric (Border 5). Join as required.*

MAKE THE BLOCKS

1. Sew B to C. Press the seam towards C.

2. Sew Br to Cr. Press the seam towards Cr.

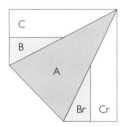

3. Sew B/C to the left long side of A. Sew Br/Cr to the right long side of A. Press the seams towards A.

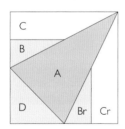

4. Sew D to the short side of A to complete the block. Make 169 blocks.

ASSEMBLE THE QUILT

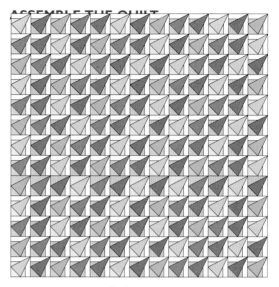

Quilt center

1. Lay the blocks out in rows across the quilt making sure their orientation is correct.

Row 1 – basic block repeated 13 times.

Repeat this row 13 times.

2. Join the blocks into rows. Press the seams of each row in the opposite direction to the previous row so that the seams can be butted when they are joined.

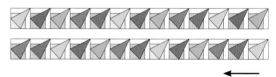

3. To complete the quilt center, join the rows, butting the seams and making sure all points and joins match.

COMPLETE THE QUILT CENTER

1. At this stage there are two edges that do not have a white border. Referring to Adding Borders with Square Corners in Techniques for Quiltmaking, page 94, measure the length of the quilt through the center. Cut a strip this length from the long 1½in white strip. Pin, then sew this strip to the left edge of the quilt center, matching centers. Press the seam allowance towards the border.

2. Measure the width of the quilt through the center. Cut a strip this length from the long 1½in white strip. Pin, then sew this strip to the bottom edge of the quilt center. Press the seam allowance towards the border.

ADD THE BORDERS

1. Referring to Adding Borders with Square Corners in Techniques for Quiltmaking on page 94, measure the width of the quilt across the center. Trim two 4½in strips of yellow floral fabric to that length, joining strips where necessary.

2. Pin, then sew a strip to the top and bottom edges of the quilt, matching centers. Press the seam allowance towards the borders.

3. In the same manner, measure the length of the quilt through the center. Trim two 4½in strips of yellow floral fabric to that length, joining strips where necessary.

4. Pin, then sew a strip to the left and right edges of the quilt, matching centers. Press the seam allowance towards the borders.

5. Repeat steps 1-4 with the 2in strips of white fabric for Border 2; with the 3in strips of pink striped fabric for Border 3; with the 2in strips of white fabric for Border 4; and with the 9½in strips of lemon floral for Border 5, joining strips where necessary.

FINISH THE QUILT

1. Cut the length of backing fabric in three. Remove the selvages. Sew the three sections together lengthwise, then trim to 98in square for the backing of the quilt.

2. Layer the backing, batting and quilt top. Pin or thread baste all the layers together.

3. Quilt as desired, either by machine or hand. *The Floral Quilt* was commercially quilted using an all-over rose pattern.

4. Bind the quilt with the 2½in strips of pink striped fabric, referring to Binding the Quilt in Techniques for Quiltmaking, page 95. Label your quilt.

Comment on Color

*Variety is the key to success for **The Floral Quilt**. Lots of different beautiful floral fabrics were used for the dominant triangle. Beg or swap 5in squares of floral fabric to get the variety you need, then match the floral fabrics with soft, tone-on-tone pastel fabrics. The background white softens the palette even more, giving a wonderful shabby chic appearance to the quilt. When adding borders as large as these, it is important to have a variety of textures, so include a stripe as well as eye-catching large floral prints.*

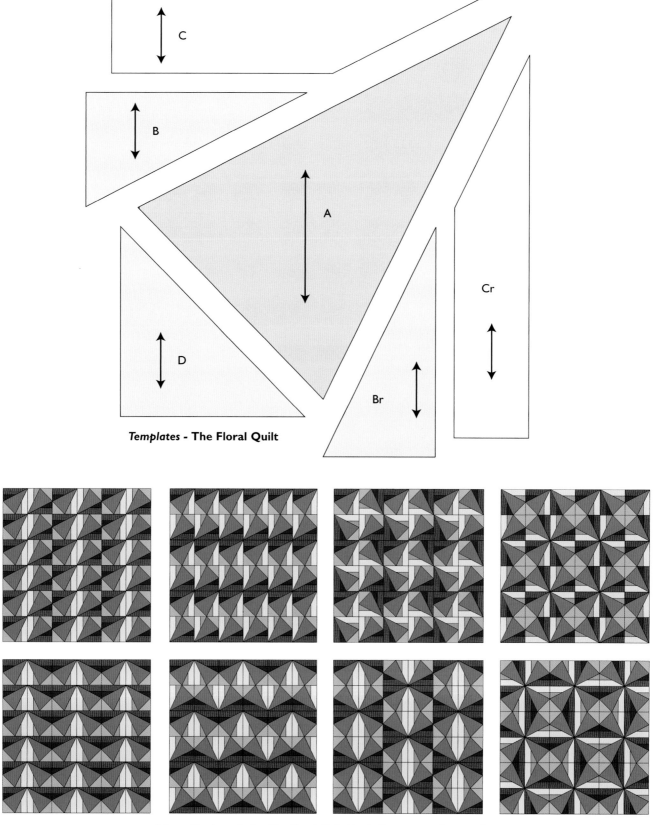

Templates - The Floral Quilt

Alternative layouts for **The Floral Quilt** block. For personal use only.

Enlarge and color to create new quilt designs for **The Floral Quilt** block. For personal use only.

Fireworks
Finished size: 31in x 31in (79cm x 79cm)
Block size: 3in (7.5cm)

Fireworks

*Fireworks is an example of **rotation**. Here, the basic block has undergone three rotations. It has been turned through 90°, 180° and 270° in a clockwise direction, giving the quilt the illusion of movement. The blocks have been placed so that the major focus of the rotation is the fabulous double-spoke Catherine Wheel at the center. However, the secondary pattern of dark purple spokes resulting from the repeat of the rotated unit of four blocks means a darkening of the quilt so that the yellow Catherine Wheels stand out even more.*

Fireworks block

Fireworks block rotated 90°

Fireworks block rotated 180°

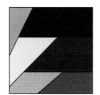
Fireworks block rotated 270°

MATERIALS

¼yd (25cm) in total of a variety of red fabrics

¼yd (25cm) in total of a variety of mustard fabrics

¼yd (25cm) in total of a variety of orange fabrics

¼yd (25cm) in total of a variety of dark brown fabrics

¼yd (25cm) in total of a variety of purple fabrics

¼yd (25cm) in total of a variety of mauve fabrics

¼yd (25cm) extra mustard fabric (Border 1)

¼yd (25cm) extra orange fabric (Border 2)

½yd (50cm) extra purple fabric (Border 3 and binding)

1¼yd (1m) backing fabric

Batting at least 39in x 39in (99cm x 99cm)

⅞yd (70cm) light weight no iron interfacing

Dressmakers' carbon

Tracing paper

Flower pins

Ballpoint pen

Neutral thread (piecing and quilting)

CUT THE FABRIC

From the extra mustard fabric, cut:
- 4 strips, 1¼in x width of fabric (Border 1)

From the extra orange fabric, cut:
- 4 strips, 1¼in x width of fabric (Border 2)

From the extra purple fabric, cut:
- 4 strips, 2in x width of fabric (Border 3)
- 4 strips, 2¼in x width of fabric (binding).

MAKE THE BLOCKS

1. Referring to Making Blocks with Foundations in Techniques for Quiltmaking, page 93, prepare foundations for 64 blocks using the *Fireworks* Foundation Diagram below.

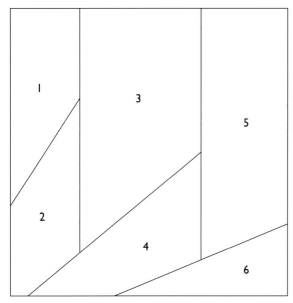

Foundation for *Fireworks* block

2. Remember when working on foundations that it is best to overestimate the size of the fabric required for each shape, then trim away the excess after stitching. Remember to sew on the **wrong** (marked) side of the foundation with the fabric pieces on the right (unmarked) side of the foundation.

3. Pin shape 1 in brown with its wrong side to the right (unmarked) side of the foundation. See Step 1 in Making Blocks with Foundations, page 93.

4. Pin shape 2 in orange with its right side facing the right side of shape 1. Turn the foundation over. Stitch along the seam line between shape 1 and shape 2 on the foundation, extending the stitching into the seam allowance at the start and finish of the seam. Turn the foundation back. Trim away any excess seam allowance. Push shape 2 back over the seam, finger press and pin it in place. See Step 2 in Making Blocks with Foundations, page 93.

5. Sew shape 3 in red to the foundation in the same way. See Step 3 in Making Blocks with Foundations, page 93.

6. Sew shape 4 in mustard, shape 5 in purple and shape 6 in mauve to the foundation in the same way. Make 64 blocks.

ASSEMBLE THE QUILT

Quilt center

1. Lay the blocks out in rows across the quilt, making sure their orientation is correct.

Row 1 – basic block + block rotated 90° clockwise. Repeat four times.
Row 2 – block rotated 270° clockwise + block rotated 180° clockwise. Repeat four times.

Repeat these two rows four times.

2. Join the blocks into rows. Press the seams of each row in the opposite direction to the previous row so that the seams can be butted when they are joined.

3. Join the rows, butting the seams and making sure all points and joins match, to complete the quilt center.

ADD THE BORDERS

1. Referring to Adding Borders with Square Corners in Techniques for Quiltmaking on page 94, measure the width of the quilt across the center. Trim two 1¼in strips of extra mustard fabric to this length.

2. Pin, then sew a mustard strip to the top and bottom edges of the quilt, matching centers. Press the seam allowances towards the borders.

3. In the same manner, measure the length of the quilt through the center. Trim two 1¼in strips of extra mustard fabric to this length.

4. Pin, then sew a mustard strip to the left and right edges of the quilt, matching centers. Press the seam allowances towards the borders.

5. Repeat steps 1-4 with the 1¼in strips of extra orange fabric for Border 2 and the 2in strips of extra purple fabric for Border 3.

Comment on Color°

Rather than selecting one fabric for the center of the Catherine Wheel, it is better to select three different soft, warm colors such as orange, mauve and mustard to make the quilt more interesting.

For the dark spokes, add red and brown to the color mix rather than using one fabric. Brown is a very good color to add depth to a quilt, and here it helps the yellow spokes to reflect more light.

FINISH THE QUILT

1. Remove the selvages from the backing fabric. Trim to 39in square for the backing of the quilt.

2. Layer the backing, batting and quilt top. Pin or thread-baste all the layers together.

3. Quilt as desired, either by machine or hand. Finding an interesting way to quilt a rotated block quilt is a challenge because the patchwork pattern is the most important design element and the quilting must not detract from it. *Fireworks* was machine quilted with a simple grid, using the seam lines as a guide.

Quilting Design for *Fireworks*

4. Bind the quilt with 2¼in strips of extra purple fabric, referring to Binding the Quilt in Techniques for Quiltmaking on page 95. Label your quilt.

For alternative color layouts for *Fireworks,* see page 70. For new quilt designs for you to enlarge and color, see page 70.

Shadehouse
Finished size: *31in x 31in (79cm x 79cm)*
Block size: *3in (7.5cm)*

Shadehouse

*This design uses **reflection** only. The basic block is used with its **vertical reflection**. Only plain fabrics are used to construct the blocks creating an exciting and vibrant design.*

Shadehouse block   Vertical reflection of
Shadehouse block

MATERIALS

*2yd (2m) in total of a wide variety of plain
fabrics*

*¼yd (20cm) black and white striped fabric
(Border 1)*

*¼yd (20cm) each of pink, gold, brown and
turquoise plain fabric (Border 2 and
binding)*

1¼yd (1m) backing fabric

Batting at least 39in x 39in (99cm x 99cm)

⅞yd (70cm) light weight no iron interfacing

Dressmakers' carbon

Tracing paper

Flower pins

Ballpoint pen

Neutral thread for piecing and hand quilting

CUT THE FABRIC

From the striped fabric, cut:
- *4 strips, 1¼in x width of fabric (Border 1)*

From each of the pink, yellow, turquoise and brown fabrics, cut:
- *1 strip, 3¼in x width of fabric (Border 2)*
- *1 strip, 2¼in x width of fabric (binding)*

MAKE THE BLOCKS

1. Referring to Making Blocks with Foundations in Techniques for Quiltmaking, page 93, prepare foundations for 32 basic blocks and 32 reflected blocks using the *Shadehouse* Foundation Diagrams on page 68.

2. Remember when working on foundations, that it is best to overestimate the size of the fabric required for each shape, then trim away the excess after stitching. Remember to sew on the **wrong** (marked) side of the foundation with the fabric pieces on the right (unmarked) side of the foundation.

3. Pin shape 1 in a darker color with its wrong side to the right (unmarked) side of the foundation. See Step 1 in Making Blocks with Foundations, page 93.

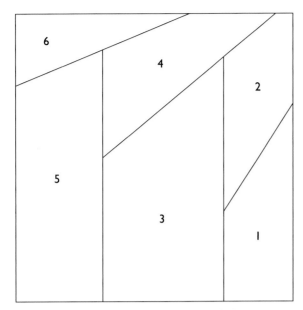

Foundation for *Shadehouse* block

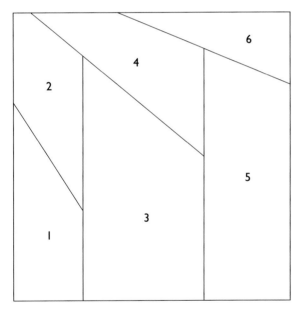

Foundation for reflected *Shadehouse* block

4. Pin shape 2 in a lighter color with its right side facing the right side of shape 1. Turn the foundation over. Stitch along the seam line between shapes 1 and 2 on the foundation, extending the stitching into the seam allowance at the start and finish of the seam. Turn the foundation back. Trim away any excess seam allowance. Push shape 2 back over the seam, finger press and pin it in place. See Step 2 in Making Blocks with Foundations, page 93.

5. Sew shape 3 in a darker color to the foundation in the same way. See Step 3 in Making Blocks with Foundations, page 93.

6. Sew shape 4 in a lighter color, shape 5 in a darker color and shape 6 in a lighter color to the foundation in the same way. Make 32 basic blocks and 32 reflected blocks.

ASSEMBLE THE QUILT

Quilt center

1. Lay the blocks out in rows across the quilt, making sure their orientation is correct.

Row 1 – basic block + vertically reflected block. Repeat four times.
Row 2 – vertically reflected block + basic block. Repeat four times.

Repeat these two rows four times.

2. Join the blocks into rows. Press the seams of each row in the opposite direction to the previous row so that the seams can be butted when the rows are joined.

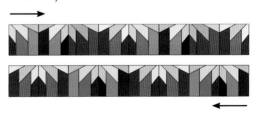

3. To complete the quilt center, join the rows, butting the seams and making sure all points and joins match.

ADD BORDER I

1. Referring to Adding Borders with Square Corners in Techniques for Quiltmaking on page 94, measure the width of the quilt across the center. Trim two 1¼in strips of striped fabric to that length.

2. Pin, then sew a striped strip to the top and bottom edges of the quilt, matching centers. Press the seam allowance towards the borders.

3. In the same manner, measure the length of the quilt through the center. Trim two 1¼in strips of striped fabric to that length.

4. Pin, then sew a striped strip to the left and right edges of the quilt, matching centers. Press the seam allowance towards the border.

ADD BORDER 2

1. Join the 3¼in strips of pink and yellow fabrics end to end. Similarly, join the 3¼in strips of turquoise and brown fabrics.

2. Referring to Adding Borders with Square Corners in Techniques for Quiltmaking on page 94, measure the width of the quilt across the center. Keeping in mind that the seam needs to be placed in a pleasing position on the border and using the quilt photo as a guide, trim the ends off the pink and yellow strip to that width for the bottom border. Similarly, trim the ends of the turquoise and brown strip to that width for the top border. Save the cut-off pieces for the side borders.

3. Pin, then sew the pink and yellow strip to the bottom edge of the quilt and the turquoise and brown strip to the top edge of the quilt, matching centers. Press the seam allowance towards the border.

4. Join the remnants of the brown and yellow strips and the remnants of the turquoise and pink strips. Measure the length of the quilt through the center and trim the brown and yellow strip and the turquoise and pink strip to that length, again taking note of where the join will be on the border.

5. Pin, then sew the yellow and brown strip to the right edge of the quilt, matching centers and with the yellow section joining the yellow section on the bottom border.

6. Pin, then sew the turquoise and pink border to the left edge of the quilt, matching centers and with the turquoise section joining the turquoise section on the top border. Press the seam allowances towards the border.

FINISH THE QUILT

1. Remove the selvages from the backing fabric. Trim to 39in square for the backing of the quilt.

2. Layer the backing, batting and quilt top. Pin or thread baste all the layers together.

3. Quilt as desired, either by machine or hand. *Shadehouse* was hand quilted using a random spiral, connected with vertical lines.

4. Join the 2½in strips of pink, yellow, turquoise and brown fabric end to end. Bind the quilt referring to Binding the Quilt in Techniques for Quiltmaking on page 95 and taking care to place the colors in a different position from where they appear in Border 2. Label your quilt.

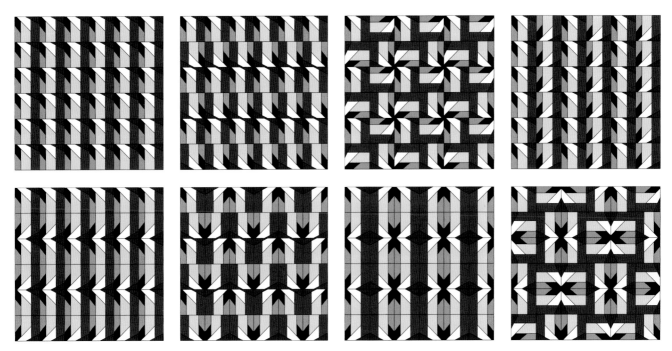

Alternative color layouts for the *Fireworks* and *Shadehouse* blocks.

Enlarge and color to create new quilt designs for *Fireworks* and *Shadehouse* blocks. For personal use only.

Waves

Waves *uses both* **rotation** *and* **reflection** *in its vibrant design that has both movement and energy. Here the basic block has undergone three changes, a 90° clockwise rotation, a vertical reflection and a 270° rotation of the reflected block.*

Waves block

180° rotation of Waves block

Horizontally reflected Waves block

Horizontally reflected Waves block rotated 180°

MATERIALS

½yd (50cm) in total of a variety of yellow fabrics

½yd (50cm) in total of a variety of red fabrics

½yd (50cm) in total of a variety of grey fabrics

½yd (50cm) in total of a variety of white with black fabrics

½yd (50cm) in total of a variety of black with white fabrics

¼yd (20cm) black and white checked fabric (Border 1)

½yd (50cm) extra red fabric (Border 2 and binding)

1¼yd (1m) backing fabric

Batting at least 39in x 39in (99cm x 99cm)

¾yd (70cm) light weight no iron interfacing

Dressmakers' carbon

Tracing paper

Flower pins

Ballpoint pen

Neutral thread (piecing and quilting)

CUT THE FABRIC

From the black and white checked fabric, cut:
- 4 strips, 1¼in x width of fabric (Border 1)

From the extra red fabric, cut:
- 4 strips, 3¼in x width of fabric (Border 2)
- 4 strips, 2½in x width of fabric (binding).

Waves

Finished size: 31in x 31in (79cm x 79cm)

Block size: 3in (7.5cm)

MAKE THE BLOCKS

1. Referring to Making Blocks with Foundations in Techniques for Quiltmaking, page 93, prepare foundations for 32 basic blocks and 32 reflected blocks using the *Waves* Foundation Diagrams below.

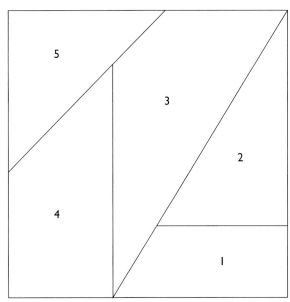

Foundation for *Waves* block

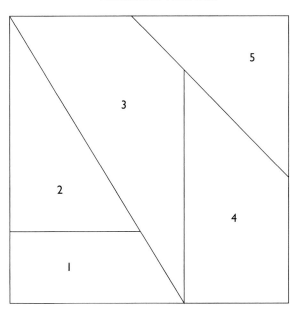

Foundation for reflected *Waves* block

2. Remember when working on foundations that it is best to overestimate the size of the fabric required for each shape, then trim away the excess after stitching. Remember to sew on the **wrong** (marked) side of the foundation with the fabric pieces on the right (unmarked) side of the foundation.

3. Pin shape 1 in grey with its wrong side to the right (unmarked) side of the foundation. See Step 1 in Making Blocks with Foundations, page 93.

4. Pin shape 2 in yellow with its right side facing the right side of shape 1. Turn the foundation over. Stitch along the seam line between shapes 1 and 2 on the foundation, extending the stitching into the seam allowance at the start and finish of the seam. Turn the foundation back. Trim away any excess seam allowance. Push shape 2 back over the seam, finger press and pin it in place. See Step 2 in Making Blocks with Foundations, page 93.

5. Sew shape 3 in white, shape 4 in black and shape 5 in red to the foundation in the same way. Make 32 basic blocks and 32 reflected blocks.

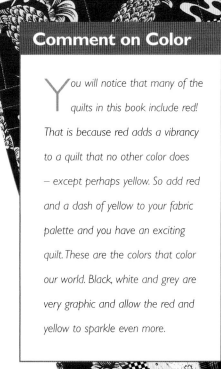

Comment on Color

You will notice that many of the quilts in this book include red! That is because red adds a vibrancy to a quilt that no other color does – except perhaps yellow. So add red and a dash of yellow to your fabric palette and you have an exciting quilt. These are the colors that color our world. Black, white and grey are very graphic and allow the red and yellow to sparkle even more.

ASSEMBLE THE QUILT

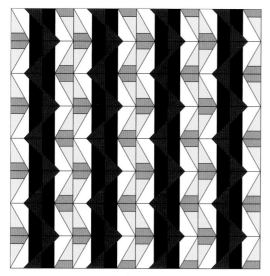

Quilt center

1. Lay the blocks out in rows across the quilt, making sure their orientation is correct.

Row 1 – basic block + 180° rotation of the basic block. Repeat four times.
Row 2 – horizontal reflection of the basic block + 180° clockwise rotation of the horizontally reflected block.

Repeat these two rows four times.

2. Join the blocks into rows. Press the seams of each row in the opposite direction to the previous row so the seams can be butted when the rows are joined.

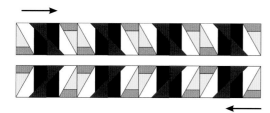

3. To complete the quilt center, join the rows, butting the seams and making sure all points and joins match.

ADD THE BORDERS

1. Referring to Adding Borders with Square Corners in Techniques for Quiltmaking on page 94 measure the width of the quilt across the center. Trim two 1¼in strips of black and white check fabric to that length.

2. Pin, then sew a checked strip to the top and bottom edges of the quilt, matching centers. Press the seam allowance towards the borders.

3. In the same manner, measure the length of the quilt through the center. Trim the remaining two 1¼in strips of black and white checked fabric to this length.

4. Pin, then sew a checked strip to the left and right edges of the quilt, matching centers. Press the seam allowance towards the borders.

5. Repeat steps 1-4 with the 3¼in strips of extra red fabric for Border 2.

FINISH THE QUILT

1. Remove the selvages from the backing fabric. Trim to 39in square for the backing of the quilt.

2. Layer the backing, batting and quilt top. Pin or thread baste all the layers together.

3. Quilt as desired, either by machine or hand. *Waves* was machine quilted in a zigzag pattern following the lines of the quilt.

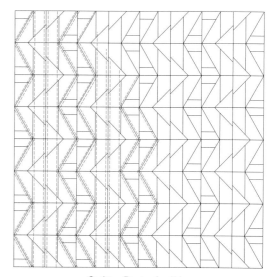

Quilting Design for *Waves*

4. Bind the quilt with 2½in strips of extra red fabric, referring to Binding the Quilt in Techniques for Quiltmaking on page 95. Label your quilt.

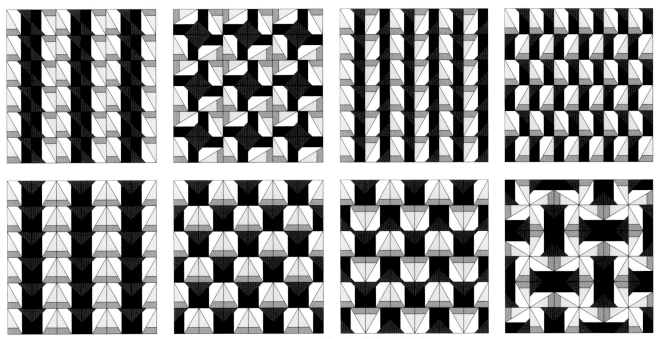

Alternative layouts for the *Waves* block.

Enlarge and color to create new quilt designs for the *Waves* block. For personal use only.

Red Ikat
Finished size: 46in x 46in (117cm x 117cm)
Block size: 6in (15cm)

Red Ikat

This quilt design features **rotation** of the block.
The block is rotated through 180° clockwise with a column
of rotated blocks placed beside a column of basic blocks.

Red Ikat block   Red Ikat block
rotated 180°

MATERIALS

1½yd (1.4m) red ikat fabric
   (Template B, Border 2 and binding)
½yd (40cm) each of two other red fabrics
   (Template B)
½yd (40cm) peach fabric (Template A and
   D)
½yd (40cm) ochre hand-dyed fabric
   (Template A and D)
½yd (40cm) mauve tone-on-tone fabric
   (Template A and D)
½yd (40cm) orange fabric (Template E)
½yd (40cm) dark grey fabric (Template C)
¼yd (25cm) purple striped fabric (Border 1)
3yd (2.8m) backing fabric
Batting at least 54in x 54in (137cm x
   137cm)
Tracing paper
Flower pins
Neutral thread
Perle No. 12 thread in a shade to match
   (optional for hand quilting)
Chenille needle (optional for hand quilting
   with Perle thread)

CUT THE FABRIC

Note:

*i) The templates are on page 80. Detailed instructions are given
for Preparing Templates and Using Templates in Techniques for
Quiltmaking on page 92. Remember the templates provided do* **not**
include a seam allowance.

*ii) Although instructions are given for cutting out the whole quilt, it
is preferable to cut out and make up one block first to confirm the
accuracy of your piecing.*

From the red ikat fabric, cut:

- 5 strips, 4in x width of fabric (Border 2)
- 12 Template B. Remember to place the template **right side up**
  on the **right side** of the fabric, securing with flower pins. Lay the
  ruler with the ¼in line against one side of the template and cut
  along the ruler. Repeat for all sides of the template.

From each of the two other red fabrics, cut:

- 12 Template B

From each of the peach, ochre and mauve fabrics, cut:

- 12 Template A
- 12 Template D

From the orange fabric, cut:

- 36 Template E

From the dark grey fabric, cut:

- 36 Template C

From the purple striped fabric, cut:

- 4 strips, 1¾in x width of fabric (Border 1)

MAKE THE BLOCKS

1. One of the features of this quilt is the color change across the quilt. This is achieved by making three different sections of twelve blocks arranged in columns. The blocks are **rotated** through 180° in the second column of each section.

For Section 1 (on left):
　　　　Template A, D – peach
　　　　Template B – red (not ikat)
　　　　Template C – dark grey
　　　　Template E – orange

For Section 2 (in center):
　　　　Template A, D – ochre
　　　　Template B – red (ikat)
　　　　Template C – dark grey
　　　　Template E – orange

For Section 3 (on right):
　　　　Template A, D – mauve
　　　　Template B – red (not ikat)
　　　　Template C – dark grey
　　　　Template E – orange

2. For each block, taking note of the color combinations required for each section of the blocks.

Sew C to D. Press the seam towards D.

3. Sew C/D to the left side of B. Press the seam towards B.

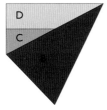

4. Sew A to the right side of B. Press the seam towards B.

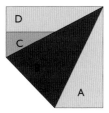

5. Finally, add E to the short side of B to complete the *Red Ikat* block. Make 12 blocks using the color combination for Section 1, 12 blocks for Section 2 and 12 blocks for Section 3.

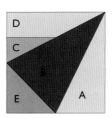

ASSEMBLE THE QUILT

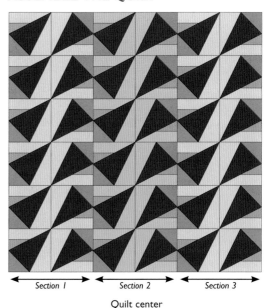

Quilt center

1. Lay out the blocks for each section in columns.

For Section 1 (using blocks with peach background)
Column 1 – six basic blocks
Column 2 – six blocks rotated 180°

For Section 2 (using blocks with ochre background)
Column 1 – six basic blocks
Column 2 – six blocks rotated 180°

For Section 3 (using blocks with mauve background)
Column 1 – six basic blocks
Column 2 – six blocks rotated 180°

2. Join the blocks into columns. Press the seams of each column in the opposite direction to the previous column so that the seams can be butted when the columns are joined.

2. To complete the quilt center, join the columns, butting the seams and making sure all points and joins match.

ADD THE BORDERS

1. Referring to Adding Borders with Square Corners in Techniques for Quiltmaking on page 94, measure the width of the quilt across the center. Trim two 1¾in strips of purple striped fabric to that length.

2. Pin, then sew a strip to the top and bottom edges of the quilt, matching centers. Press the seam allowances towards the borders.

3. In the same manner, measure the length of the quilt through the center. Trim two 1¾in strips of purple striped fabric to that length.

4. Pin, then sew a strip to the left and right edges of the quilt, matching centers. Press the seam allowances towards the borders.

5. Repeat steps 1-4 for the 4in strips of red ikat fabric for Border 2, joining the strips as required.

FINISH THE QUILT

1. Cut the length of backing fabric in half. Remove the selvages. Join the two sections together lengthwise, then trim to 54in square for the backing of the quilt.

2. Layer the backing, batting and quilt top. Pin or thread baste all the layers together.

3. Quilt as desired, either by machine or hand. *Red Ikat* was hand quilted with zigzag lines across the quilt and straight lines from top to bottom using Perle No.12 thread. When hand quilting with Perle No. 12 thread, use a small chenille needle rather than a quilting needle because it is much stronger.

Quilting Design for *Red Ikat*

3. Bind the quilt with 2¼in strips of extra purple fabric, referring to Binding the Quilt in Techniques for Quiltmaking on page 95. Label your quilt.

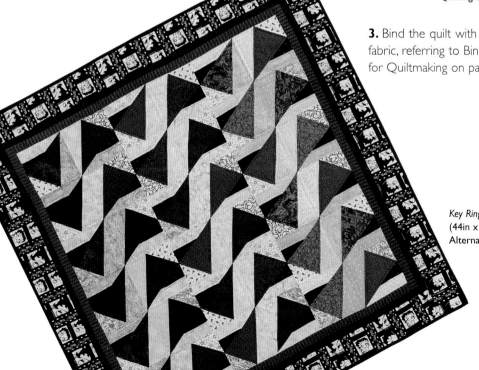

Key Ring by Carolyn Sullivan
(44in x 44in)
Alternative colorway for *Red Ikat*.

Red Ikat

Templates - Red Ikat

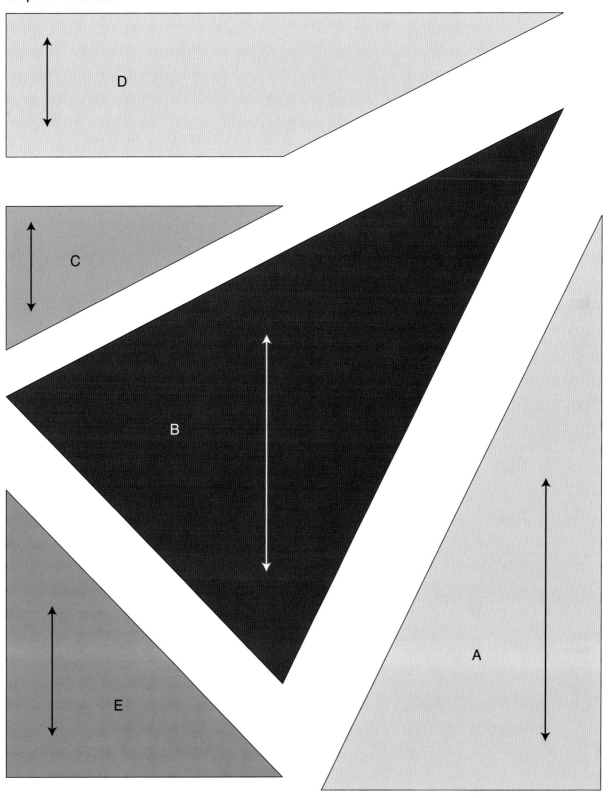

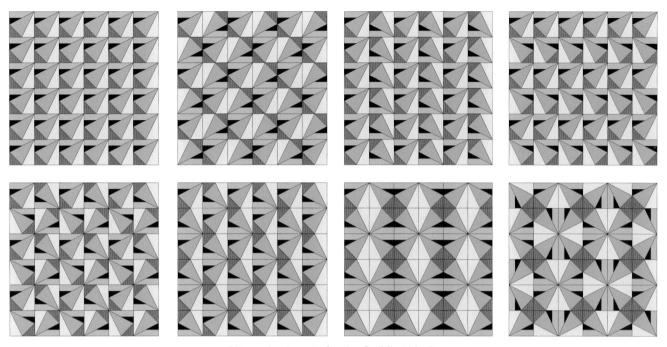

Alternative layouts for the **Red Ikat** block

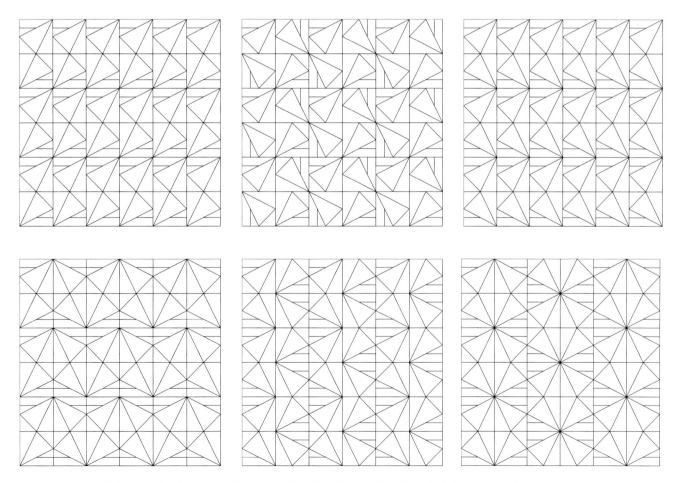

Enlarge and color to create new quilt designs for the **Red Ikat** block. For personal use only.

Underneath the Arches
Finished size: 79in x 79in (202cm x 202cm)
Block size: 5½in x 7¾in (14cm x 20cm)

Underneath the Arches

This quilt is very different from the other quilts in this book because it has been cut using a free cutting method rather than using templates or foundations. It is also based on a rectangle rather than a square, showing that the rules that have been applied to squares are just as easily carried over to a rectangle. Rather than follow through with design work, the fabric is cut spontaneously for the basic block then cut in the opposite direction for the reflected block. While not strictly a mirror image, the combination creates an exciting design.

MATERIALS

108 rectangles, 9½in x 11in of a large variety of bright prints, both light and dark
1¾yd (1.7m) striped fabric (center cross, Border 1, binding)
1yd (1m) in total of a variety of prints (Border 2)
7¼yd (6.7m) backing fabric
Batting at least 87in x 87in (222cm x 222cm)
Neutral thread
Rotary cutter, ruler and cutting board

CUT THE FABRIC

From the striped fabric, cut:
- *12 strips, 2¾in x width of fabric (sashing, Border 1)*
- *9 strips, 2½in x width of fabric (binding).*

From the variety of prints for Border 2, cut:
- *strips 5½in wide*

MAKE THE BLOCKS

1. Layer three bright print rectangles on top of one another. Using the rotary cutter, make two free-hand cuts through the layers.

2. Move the pieces to create three blocks with different colors in each layer. Place a pin on either side of the cuts in at least two places on both curves for each block.

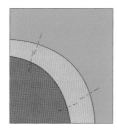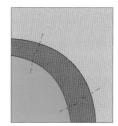

3. Matching the pins, stitch the curves on all three blocks. Press all the seams in the same direction. Clip the seams if necessary. Don't worry that the block is very distorted with unmatched edges. This has happened because there was no allowance made for seams.

4. Repeat this process with two more sets of three rectangles. Make nine blocks altogether.

5. From these nine blocks, select three blocks with nine different fabrics in them. Layer these on top of one another making sure that the seams are all aligned in the same way. Make another cut in the opposite direction.

6. Repeat this process for the two remaining sets of three blocks.

7. Lay out these pieces for nine new blocks. Try to ensure that each new block uses a different selection of fabrics. Place pins on either side of the cuts in at least two places on the curve. Matching the pins, as before, stitch the seams on all nine blocks. Note that none of the curved seams match. This is one of the joys of *Underneath the Arches*.

8. Trim away the excess fabric reducing each block to 8¼in x 6in. Note that there is quite a bit of fabric to cut away and this can be saved to make another quilt. Make 54 blocks. Only 48 blocks are required for the quilt. Use the extra blocks on the back of the quilt or for a small quilt.

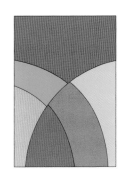

9. Make another 54 blocks cutting the curves in the opposite direction for the 'reflected' block. Remember only 48 are actually required for the quilt.

ASSEMBLE THE QUILT

Quadrant I layout diagram

I. Each quadrant of the quilt has 12 blocks with the curved seams in one direction and 12 blocks with the curved seams in the opposite direction. Lay the blocks out in rows making sure the orientation is correct and there is a good balance of color. The rectangular blocks are placed so that their long side is vertical.

Row I – basic block + reflected block. Repeat three times.
Row 2 – reflected block + basic block. Repeat three times.

Repeat these two rows twice for Quadrant 1.

2. Join the rectangular blocks into rows. Press the seams of each row in the opposite direction to the previous row so that the seams can be butted as the rows are joined.

3. Join the rows, making sure that all points and joins match to complete Quadrant 1. Make four quadrants.

4. Measure the length of Quadrant 1 through the center and trim one 2¾in strip of striped fabric to that length for the sashing. Pin, then sew it to the right hand edge of Quadrant 1, matching centers. Press the seam allowance towards the striped fabric.

5. Sew Quadrant 2 to the right edge of the striped fabric, making sure that the rows of both quadrants match visually across the sashing strip. Press the seam allowance toward the sashing.

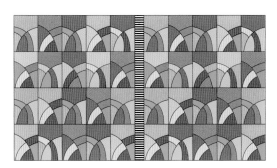

6. Repeat steps 4-5 for Quadrants 3 and 4.

7. Measure the width of both sections through the center to confirm that they are the same width. Join two 2¾in strips of striped fabric end to end and trim to that length. Pin, then sew the strip to the bottom edge of the upper section (Quadrants 1 and 2) of the quilt, matching centers. Pin, then sew the strip to the top edge of the bottom section (Quadrants 3 and 4) of the quilt. Press the seam allowance towards the striped fabric.

ADD BORDER 1

1. Join two strips of 2¾in striped fabric end to end. Repeat three times to make four long strips of striped fabric for Border 1.

2. Referring to Adding Borders with Square Corners in Techniques for Quiltmaking on page 94, measure the width of the quilt across the center of the quilt. Trim two long strips of striped fabric to that length. Pin, then sew the strips to the top and

bottom edges of the quilt, matching centers. Press the seam allowances towards the borders.

3. Measure the length of the quilt through the center of the quilt. Trim two long strips of striped fabric to that length. Pin, then sew them to the right and left edges of the quilt, matching centers. Press the seam allowances towards the borders.

ADD BORDER 2

1. Join several strips of a variety of 5½in wide Border 2 fabrics end to end. To join the strips, lay two strips to be cut on top of one another so that there is a small overlap and cut a free curve through both layers of fabric. Sew them together in the same way as the curved seams in the blocks. Note that in *Underneath the Arches*, several fabrics have been used in each border strip. Make four long strips at least 80in long for Border 2.

2. Referring to Adding Borders with Square Corners in Techniques for Quiltmaking on page 94, measure the width of the quilt across the center of the quilt. Trim two long strips of Border 2 fabrics to that length. Pin, then sew the strips to the top and bottom edges of the quilt, matching centers. Press the seam allowances towards the borders.

3. Measure the length of the quilt through the center of the quilt. Trim two long strips of Border 2 fabrics to that length. Pin, then sew the strips to the right and left edges of the quilt, matching centers. Press the seam allowances towards the borders.

FINISH THE QUILT

1. Cut the backing into three equal lengths and remove the selvages. Sew the sections together lengthwise and trim to 87in x 87in for the backing of the quilt.

2. Layer the backing, batting and quilt top. Pin or thread baste all the layers together.

3. Quilt as desired. *Underneath the Arches* was hand quilted in a random spiral using quilting thread. (See *Shadehouse* quilting design on page 69.)

4. Bind the quilt using 2½in strips of striped fabric referring to Binding the Quilt in Techniques for Quiltmaking, page 95. Label your quilt.

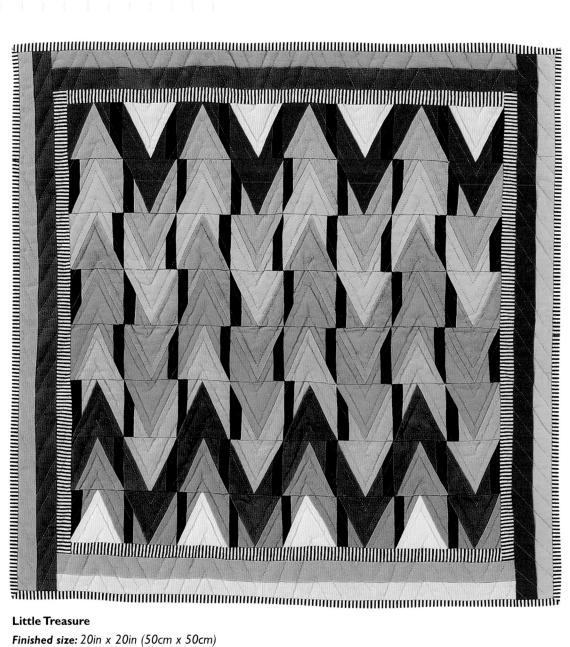

Little Treasure

Finished size: 20in x 20in (50cm x 50cm)

Block size: 2in (5cm)

Little Treasure

*Little Treasure was designed using both **reflection** and **rotation**.*

This design is not for the faint hearted as each row is colored differently.

Little Treasure block

Little Treasure block rotated 180°

Horizontal reflection of Little Treasure block

Vertical reflection of Little Treasure block

MATERIALS

¼yd (20cm) each of yellow, blue, purple, orange, turquoise, pink, green, light blue, dark pink, beige and navy plain fabrics

½yd (40cm) striped fabric (Border 1 and binding)

1yd (70cm) backing fabric

Batting at least 28in x 28in (70cm x 70cm)

¾yd (70cm) light weight no iron interfacing

Dressmakers' carbon

Tracing paper

Flower pins

Ballpoint pen

Neutral thread

CUT THE FABRIC

From the striped fabric, cut:
- 3 strips, 1in x width of fabric (Border 1)
- 3 strips, 2¼in x width of fabric (binding)

From each of the mauve and purple fabrics, cut:
- 2 strips, 1¼in x width of fabric (Border 2)

From each of the green, yellow, pink and orange fabric, cut:
- 1 strip, 1¼in x width of fabric (Border 2)

Comment on Color

The zigzags of the highs (peaks) and lows (troughs) of the pattern have been highlighted by using a variety of colors, both light and dark. The navy fabric, used consistently throughout the quilt for the small vertical bars, provides an anchor for the design as well as highlighting the changes in direction of the pattern.

MAKE THE BLOCKS

1. Referring to Making Blocks with Foundations in Techniques for Quiltmaking, page 93, prepare foundations for 32 basic blocks and 32 reflected blocks using the *Little Treasure* Foundation Diagrams below.

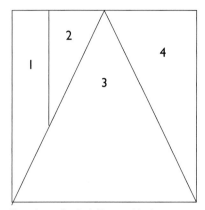

Foundation for *Little Treasure* block

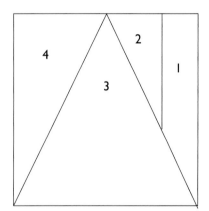

Foundation for reflected *Little Treasure* block

2. Remember when working on foundations that it is best to overestimate the size of the fabric required for each shape, then trim away the excess after stitching. Remember to sew on the **wrong** (marked) side of the foundation with the fabric shapes on the right (unmarked) side of the foundation.

3. Each row of this quilt needs to be made separately as the color changes in every row. Shape 1 is the only color that is constant throughout the quilt. Use navy fabric for this shape in every block.

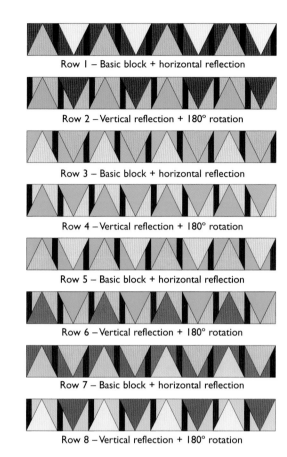

Row 1 – Basic block + horizontal reflection

Row 2 – Vertical reflection + 180° rotation

Row 3 – Basic block + horizontal reflection

Row 4 – Vertical reflection + 180° rotation

Row 5 – Basic block + horizontal reflection

Row 6 – Vertical reflection + 180° rotation

Row 7 – Basic block + horizontal reflection

Row 8 – Vertical reflection + 180° rotation

4. Pin shape 1 in navy with its wrong side to the right (unmarked) side of the foundation. See Step 1 in Making Blocks with Foundations, page 93. For every other shape, the color will depend on the row number and block position. Refer to the diagram for each row before making the blocks for that row.

5. Lay shape 2 (the color is dependent on the row number and the block position) with its right side facing the right side of shape 1. Turn the foundation over. Stitch along the seam line between shapes 1 and 2 on the foundation, extending the stitching into the seam allowance at the start and finish of the seam. Turn the foundation back. Trim away any excess seam allowance. Push shape 2 back over the seam, finger press and pin it in place. See Step 2 in Making Blocks with Foundations, page 93.

6. Sew shapes 3 and 4 to the foundation in the same way.

7. Make all the blocks following the row diagrams carefully for color selection and orientation. Make 32 blocks using the basic block foundation and 32 using the reflected block foundation.

ASSEMBLE THE QUILT

Quilt center

1. Lay the blocks out in rows across the quilt paying special attention to the orientation and color of each block according to the row diagrams.

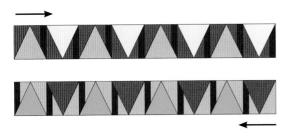

2. Join the blocks into eight rows as indicated. Press the seams of each row in the opposite direction to the previous row so that the seams can be butted together when the rows are joined.

3. Join the rows, making sure that all points and joins match.

ADD BORDER 1

1. Referring to Adding Borders with Square Corners in Techniques for Quiltmaking on page 94, measure the width of the quilt across the center of the quilt. Trim two 1in strips of striped fabric to that length.

2. Pin, then sew a striped strip to the top and bottom edge of the quilt, matching centers. Press the seam allowances towards the borders.

3. In the same manner, measure the length of the quilt through the center of the quilt. Trim two 1in strips of striped fabric to that length.

4. Pin, then sew a striped strip to the left and right edges of the quilt, matching centers. Press the seam allowances towards the borders.

ADD BORDERS 2 AND 3

1. Referring to Adding Borders with Square Corners in Techniques for Quiltmaking on page 94, measure the width of the quilt across the center. Trim one 1¼in strip from each of the mauve, yellow, purple and orange strips to that length.

2. Pin, then sew the purple strip to the top edge of the quilt and the mauve strip to the bottom edge of the quilt.

3. Pin, then sew the orange strip to the top edge of the quilt and the yellow strip to the bottom edge of the quilt.

4. In the same manner, measure the length of the quilt through the center of the quilt. Trim one 1¼in strip from each of the pink, green, purple and mauve strips to that length.

5. Pin, then sew the pink strip to the right edge of the quilt and the purple strip to the left edge of the quilt. Press the seam allowance towards the borders.

6. Pin, then sew the green strip to the right edge of the quilt and the mauve strip to the left edge of the quilt. Press the seam allowance towards the borders.

FINISH THE QUILT

1. Remove the selvages from the backing fabric. Trim to 28in x 28in.

2. Layer the backing, batting and quilt top. Pin or thread baste all the layers together.

3. Quilt as desired, either by machine or hand. *Little Treasure* was machine quilted with a simple zigzag.

4. Bind the quilt with the 2¼in strips of striped fabric referring to Binding the Quilt in Techniques for Quiltmaking, page 95. Label your quilt.

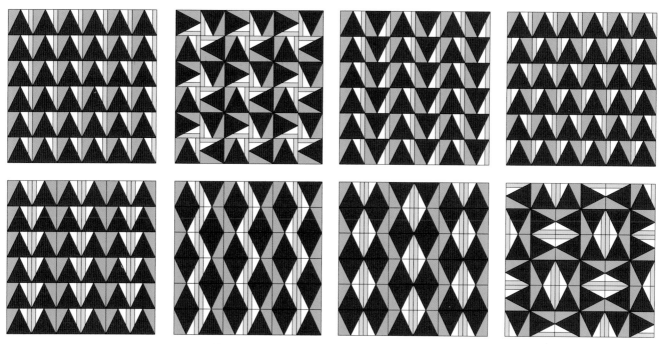

Alternative layouts for the *Little Treasure* block

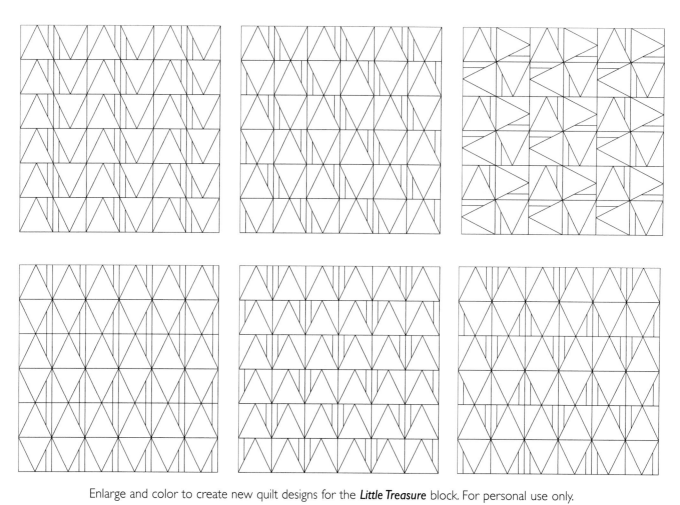

Enlarge and color to create new quilt designs for the *Little Treasure* block. For personal use only.

Techniques for Quiltmaking

PREPARING THE FABRIC

Knowing a little about the fabric we use is important. It is best to use cotton fabrics because they are easier to work with. However, if there is a fabric that you really love that is not cotton and it has a place in a quilt, then that is the fabric to use. It is best to avoid knitted fabrics as they have too much stretch.

It is important to pre-wash fabric in order to remove the chemicals that are used to finish the fabrics, to ensure that they are colorfast and to avoid shrinkage after the quilt is made. However, there is less concern about stray dyes in the fabric and shrinkage today and some quilters quite like the small amount of stiffness that the sizing gives the fabric because it makes cutting and stitching easier.

One important thing to remember about cotton is that it has a little more 'give' across the fabric than down its length. For this reason, it is best to cut all bindings and borders across the width of the fabric so that you can use this small amount of stretch as you apply them.

SUPPLIES

Thread

The quilts in this book are multi-colored so matching a thread is impossible. It is best to use a neutral thread such as grey for the piecing. If the quilt is generally dark, use a dark grey. If the quilt is generally light, use a light grey.

For quilting, use a conventional quilting thread in the color of your choice. However, for some of the quilts, it is suggested that a Perle No.12 thread be used. This gives a bigger, heavier stitch and is generally faster to stitch.

Sewing machine

Having your sewing machine in good working order is essential. It needs to be cleaned and oiled frequently and the needle changed often.

Rotary cutting tools

It is important to have a self-healing mat for cutting on. The rotary cutter is also essential for cutting fabric. The blades must always be sharp and it is wise to have spare blades on hand. The templates used for some of the projects rely on the addition of a quarter inch seam during cutting. This means that a ruler with a clear ¼in marking is important.

Needles

Always have a supply of new sharp machine needles for your machine. For hand quilting using conventional quilting thread, a Between needle is used. However, for some of the quilts, it has been suggested that Perle No.12 be used. When stitching with this it is best to use a chenille needle. This is a stronger needle than a regular sewing needle and will take the weight of the heavier thread.

Pins

For cutting the fabric using paper templates, flower pins are very useful. Because they have a flat head, they lie flat on the fabric and allow the ruler to lie flat too. This means that the ¼in seams can be cut accurately.

TEMPLATE MATERIAL

Good quality tracing paper is used for the templates. If you just intend to trace the templates in this book, then plain paper is sufficient. If you are going to draw up a block that you have designed yourself, then ¼in grided tracing paper is best. A good quality tracing paper will ensure that enough pieces for a whole quilt can be cut with one set of templates. The tracing paper is pinned to the fabric using flower pins to cut out the fabric and at the same time add the ¼in seam allowance.

GRAINLINE

Grainline is the strong line of the vertical threads in the fabric as they run the length of the fabric. To make a quilt that lies flat when finished, it is best to work with the grainline. It has already been noted that it is best to cut bindings and borders across the fabric in order to use the bit of stretch. When piecing, however, you do not want to have that stretch in your pieces.

This applies particularly to quilts made using templates. For all the templates given in the book, the grainlines have been marked with an arrow. You should line this arrow up with the grain of the fabric.

MAKING THE BLOCKS

The design method used in the book lends itself to more than one piecing technique. The quilts are made using two techniques, except for *Underneath the Arches*, which uses a free form style of cutting. Some of the quilts are made with foundations while others use templates. However, there is no reason why you cannot change techniques. Most of the foundations are 3in. If you prefer them smaller, make them smaller. If you prefer to work with templates but only foundations are supplied, then again, enlarge to your preferred size using a photocopier and create your own templates. The techniques are adaptable.

PREPARING TEMPLATES

Using good quality tracing paper, trace the templates including all markings. **Note that all the templates provided in this book have no seam allowances.** These are added at the time of cutting. If you have designed a block, draw the block to your chosen size using ¼in gridded tracing paper. Because the grid paper has vertical lines as a guide, you can now mark the grainlines correctly on the sections of your design – the templates. Label each template with a letter or number and the name of the block. It is sensible to draw two copies – one to keep as reference and the other to cut up for templates. Once it is cut into individual templates, the shapes may look quite odd. The grainline will assist in placing the pieces on the fabric correctly and the copy will ensure correct assembly of the block.

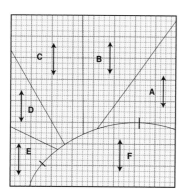

Palm Fronds block

Remember that the templates do not have a seam allowance. The seam allowance is added when cutting the fabric. The templates are the finished size of each piece.

USING TEMPLATES

1. Trace the templates provided for each block onto tracing paper. Label each template and mark the grainlines or use the templates you have made from your originally designed block.

2. Place the template **right side up** on the **right side** of the fabric, using flower pins. It is important to use these flat-headed pins so that the ruler will lie flat on the fabric. Use at least two pins for each template so that it will not move.

3. Lay the ruler with the ¼in line against the edge of

the fabric and cut along the ruler. Do this for all sides. If there is a curved seam, eyeball the seam allowance as you cut with scissors.

SEAM ALLOWANCE

Quarter inch seams are used for all the projects using templates. It is necessary to be consistent in the measurement of the ¼in so, if necessary, mark the ¼in position on the sewing machine and always work to that. Odd shaped patches, as in the projects in this book and for individually designed blocks, must be sewn together with the corners offset to ensure that the edges in the finished block are aligned. If the corners are matched and misalignment occurs, remove stitches and start again.

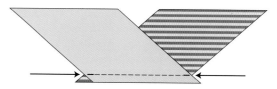

The angle indicated by the arrow is ¼in above the edges to be joined

FOUNDATIONS AND HOW TO USE THEM

Foundation piecing relies on a backing fabric onto which the patches of fabric are placed. It is a very accurate way of piecing and is particularly useful when making small blocks.

When foundation piecing, always work from the back of the work.

A soft, non-woven interfacing is best for the foundations as it is very soft to work with, easy to trace onto and does not need tearing away after stitching. There is no need to give consideration to the grain of the fabrics as the interfacing acts as a stabilizer allowing for economical use of fabric. If you prefer to machine quilt, most sewing machines handle the extra thickness of the interfacing quite well.

Making Tracings of the Foundations

1. Work with a strip of tracing paper that is at least 4in high and draw at least 4 foundations. Note that the foundations are given reversed to allow for working on the wrong side. When the block is finished, it will have the correct orientation.

Four tracings of a foundation

2. Take a strip of interfacing that is 4in wide and lay it on a flat surface. Carefully lay a 4in strip of dressmakers' carbon on top. Place another layer of interfacing and carbon on top and finally the strip of traced foundations on the tracing paper. Hold the stack in place with flower pins.

3. Using a ballpoint pen, trace the foundations again, pressing quite firmly so that the design is drawn onto the two interfacing strips.

4. Continue with this process for the required number of foundations.

Making Blocks with Foundations

When working on foundations, it is best to overestimate the size of the fabric required for each shape, then trim away the excess after stitching. Sew on the **wrong** (marked) side of the foundation with the fabric shapes on the right (unmarked) side of the foundation.

1. Accurately pin shape 1 with its wrong side to the right (unmarked) side of the foundation.

2. Lay shape 2 in place with its right side facing the right side of shape 1. Turn the foundation over. Stitch along the seam line between shape 1 and shape 2 on the foundation, extending the stitching into the seam allowance at the start and finish of the seam.

3. Turn the foundation over. Trim away any excess seam allowance. Push shape 2 back over the seam. Finger press in place.

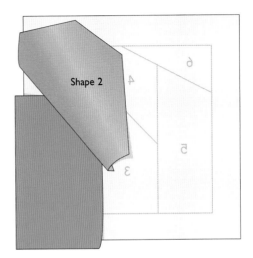

Shape 2 in place

4. Stitch shape 3 to the foundation in the same way. Turn the foundation over. Trim away any excess seam allowance. Push shape 3 back over the seam. Finger press in place.

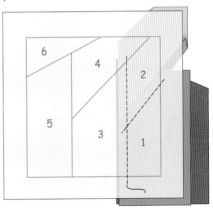

Seam between shapes (1+2) and 3.

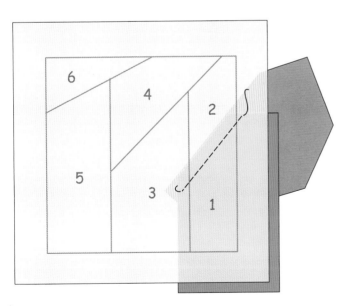

Marked (wrong) side of foundation showing the
seam between shape 1 and 2

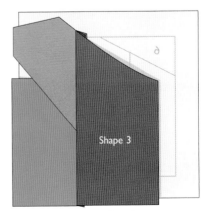

Shape 3 in place

5. Stitch shape 4 to the foundation in the same way.

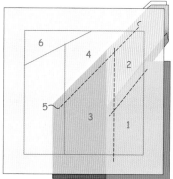

Seam between shapes (2+3) and 4

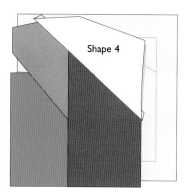

Shape 4 in place

6. Stitch shape 5 to the foundation in the same way.

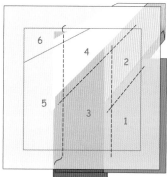

Seam between shapes (3+4) and 5

Shape 5 in place

7. Stitch shape 6 to the foundation in the same way. Trim the foundations back so that there is a ¼in seam allowance.

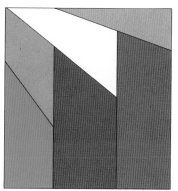

Finished block with ¼in seam allowance

ADDING BORDERS WITH SQUARE CORNERS

Borders are the fun part of the quilt as they frame and finish the quilt. Choose fabrics that complement the quilt itself, but also consider using something that gives a zing to the quilt. In **Red Ikat** (page 76), the mauve border is in contrast to the rest of the quilt, yet it is not out of place. So, too, is the blue/purple border on **In the Temple** (page 42). The blue pineapple fabric on **Palm Fronds** (page 30) completes the tropical feel of the quilt. The red pineapple fabric in **Waves** (page 71) highlights the red of the quilt.

Have as many borders as you like. Many of the quilts here have two borders, a narrow inner one and a wider outer border. But you can add more than one or two. Look at the large borders on **The Floral Quilt** (page 56). This quilt was needed for a queen sized bed, so it was enough to have the pieced part of the quilt sitting on top of the bed. The borders are the overlap. Here, there are five borders, all of different sizes.

Generally borders are added progressively. That is, the top and bottom of a border are sewn into position, then the sides are added, before the next border is added in the same way. This is the case for most of the quilts in the book. However, on **Little Treasure** (page 86) all the borders were added to the top and bottom first, then the side borders were put in place.

To determine the width of the quilt, measure the quilt across the center and cut the top and bottom borders to this length.

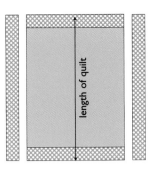

width of quilt

length of quilt

Once the top and bottom borders are added, measure the length of the quilt through the center to get the measurement for the side borders.

When attaching borders, always match the center of the border to the center of the side, then pin out to the edges. Press the seams towards the borders at each step of the way.

BINDING THE QUILT

1. To make the binding for straight edged quilts, cut lengths of fabric from selvage to selvage, 2½in wide. Join them end to end to make one long strip the length of twice the width + twice the length of the quilt. Join the strips using a straight or a bias seam.

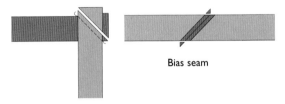

Bias seam

2. Fold and press in half along the length of the binding.

3. Pin the raw edges of the binding to an edge on the right side of the quilt. It is best not to start at a corner. Start at a seam line that is already part of the quilt if possible or a little way along an edge of the quilt. Before commencing stitching, turn under a small hem on the end of the binding so that when the binding is stitched and turned to the back of the quilt, the raw end is hidden.

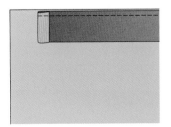

4. Pin the binding along the entire edge, stretching is very slightly as you go. Stitch along the binding, stopping at the last pin, which is at exactly the point where you want to begin the next seam. Do a small back stitch, and then cut off the threads. Fold the binding back at a 45° angle.

Fold binding back at 45°

5. Fold the binding down so that the raw edge lies along the next edge of the quilt to be bound, with the fold aligned with the top edge of the quilt. Place the first pin in the last stitch on the previous row and pin along the edge as before. Begin stitching at the first pin. Complete all sides of the quilt in the same way.

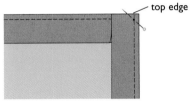

Fold binding to align with next edge

6. When the binding is attached to all four sides, turn the binding over to the back of the quilt, covering the raw edges. Make sure that the binding is filled and there is no empty space inside it. At the corners, lay one edge flat, so that a 45° angle is formed by the binding. Fold the new edge over the first and pin, then hem by hand

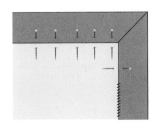

Binding pinned to the back of the quilt

QUILT LABELS

One of the most important things to remember is always to put a label on the back of your quilt. You should include your name, address, phone and email along with the title of the quilt and its completion date. You never know when you will want the information. Also, many quilters give away their quilts and it is important for future generations to know who made the quilt and where they lived.

Biography

Carolyn lives in Bundanoon, a rural township two hours out of Sydney, with her husband, Ken, and her cat, Orlando. Her much-loved children live elsewhere and this has given her the freedom to explore the world around her. She lives on five acres of flat, plateau country surrounded by eucalypt and deciduous trees in a park like site. Its cool climate, with its many gardens, closeness to the escarpment and beautiful mists, provide lots of inspiration for her work, which in recent years involves closely stitched hand work with antique silk and table linen. Her work is exhibited all over Australia and is in collections in Australia and the United States.

Her work on various committees, as president of both The Quilters' Guild NSW and Ozquilt Network, and with the Quilts 2000 project, have given her an insight into the wider picture of the Australian quilting world. It has also meant many enduring friendships with quilters all over the country.

Carolyn is a trained high school teacher who enjoys teaching people to find their own creativity and to produce stitched works that are meaning-

ful to the maker. She has travelled throughout her state of New South Wales to meet many interested students. In recent years, she has gained a Diploma in Art History from Sydney University which has encouraged her to share her knowledge and relate it to good design and conceptual thinking.

Keeping scrapbooks of her designs and thought processes is an important part of her life. These many scrapbooks are a key source of inspiration as they reference all the things she has seen and read about and all the places she has visited. By returning to them frequently, she finds ideas for design and colour for new work. She is also a frequent visitor to galleries to see how other artists are interpreting their world.

To promote her first book, **Companion Pieces**, Carolyn was a tutor at the International Quilt Festival in 1998. In **Quilted Once Block Marvels**, she further explores the ideas begun in **Companion Pieces** – making dynamic quilts from simple blocks created with a few lines as she repeats, rotates and reflects these blocks.